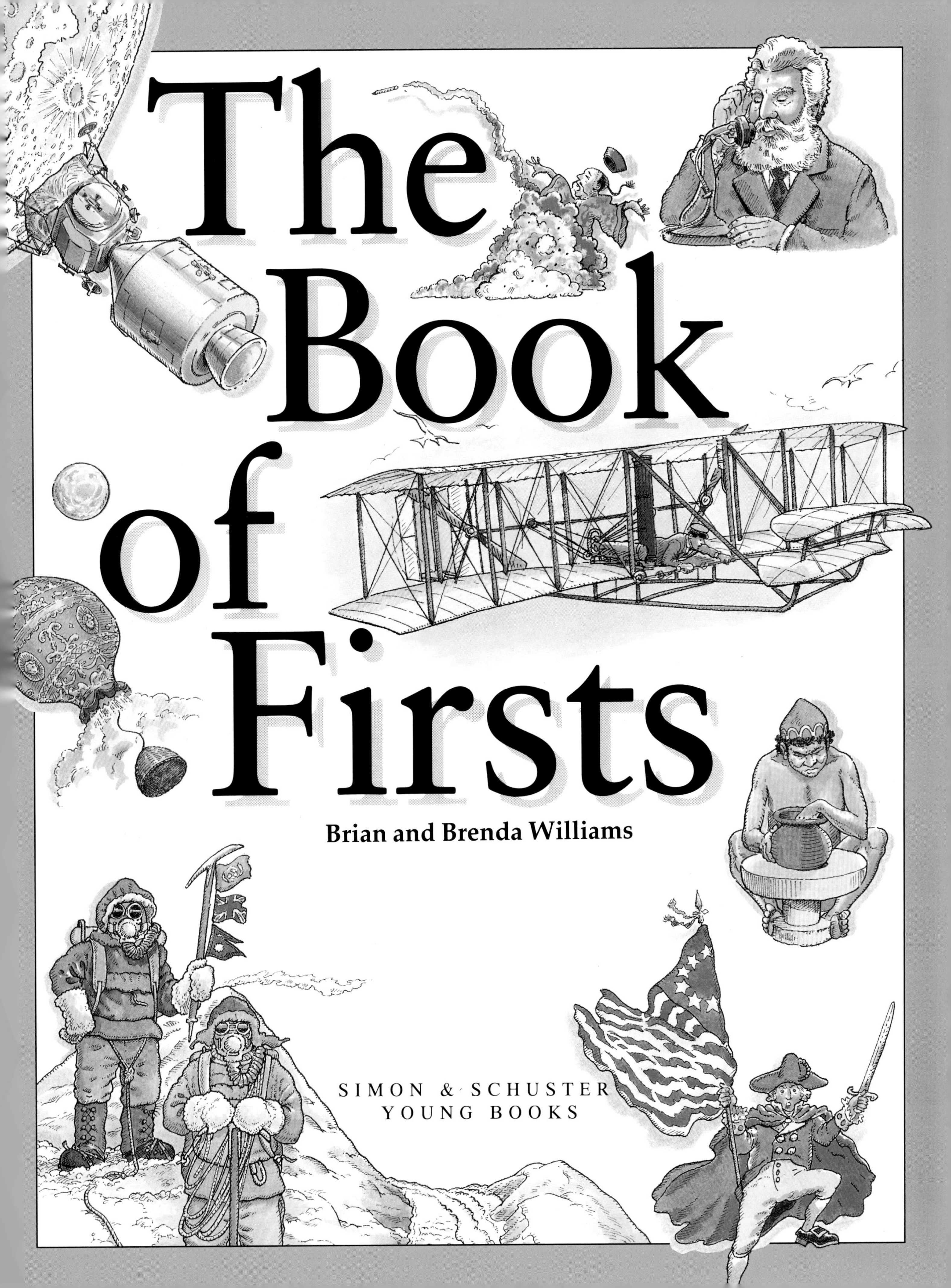

The Book of Firsts

Brian and Brenda Williams

SIMON & SCHUSTER
YOUNG BOOKS

CONTENTS

The Natural World

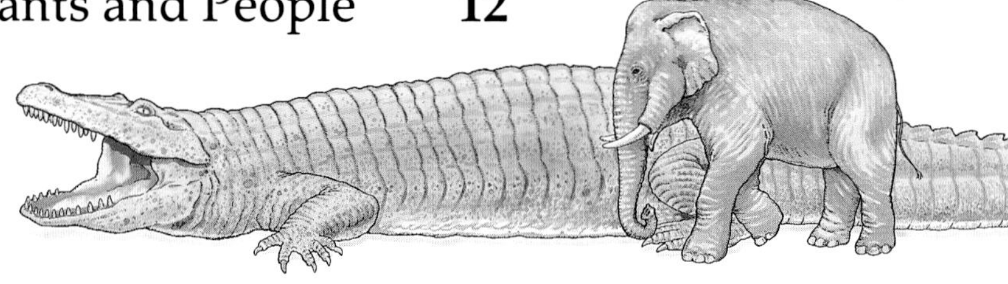

Technology

Transport

First published in 1993 by
Simon & Schuster Young Books
Campus 400
Maylands Avenue
Hemel Hempstead
Herts
HP2 7EZ

ISBN 07500 1309 5
ISBN 07500 1317 6 pb

A CIP catalogue record for this book is available from the British Library.

Senior editor Thomas Keegan
Editor Chris Norris
Designer Robert Wheeler
Illustrators Gary Rees, Jason Lewis, and Roger Fereday
Cover Design David West

Phototypeset by Goodfellow & Egan Ltd, Cambridge
Printed and bound in Hong Kong

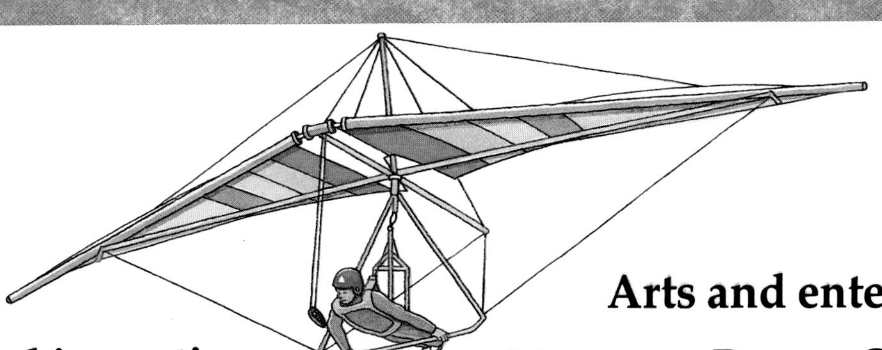

Science and invention

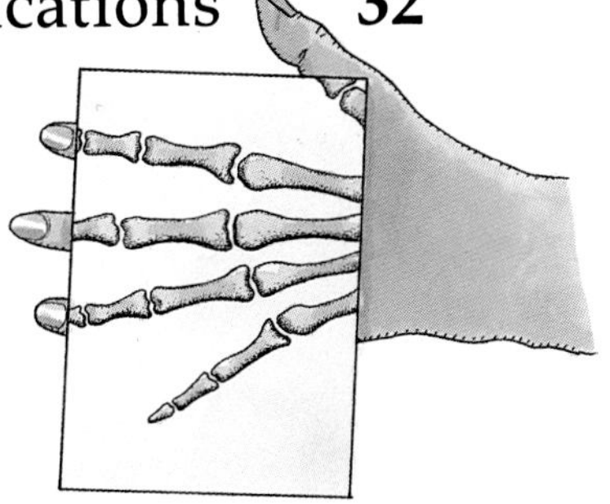

History

Exploration

Arts and entertainment

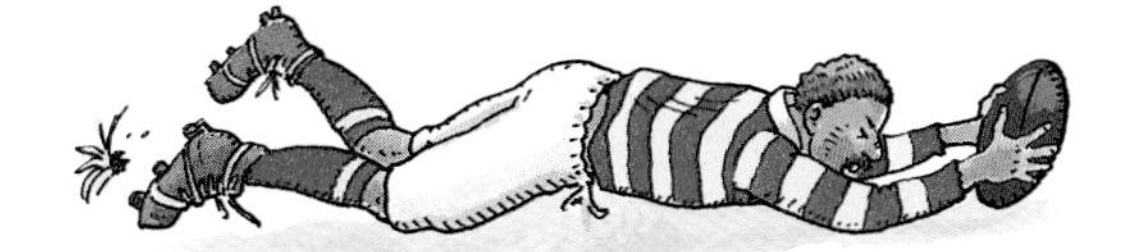

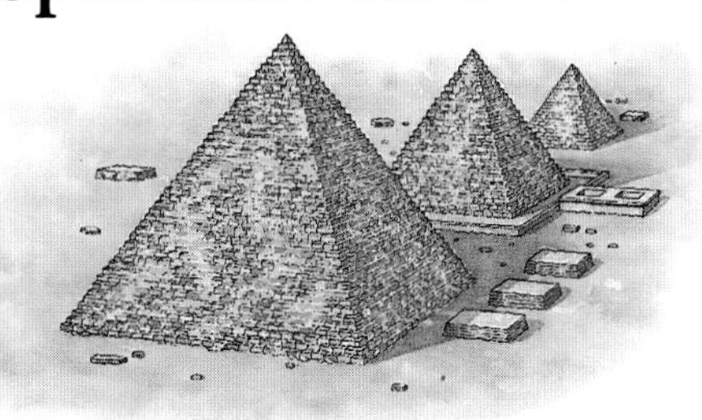

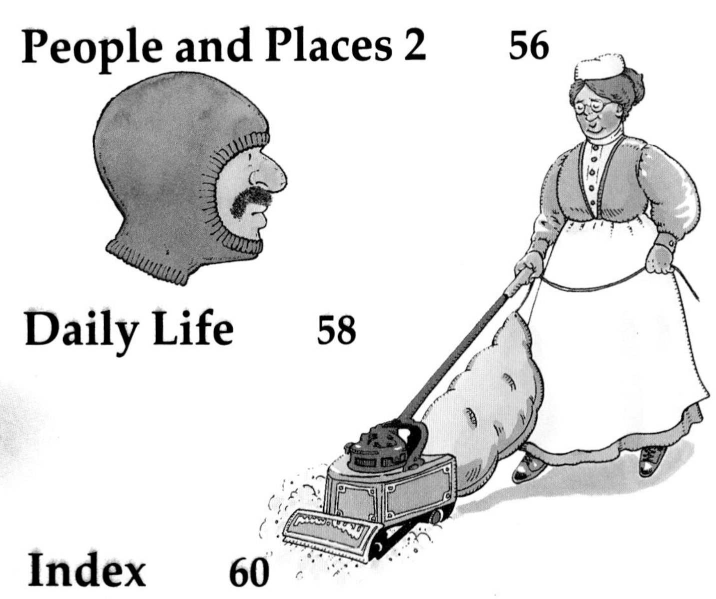

THE NATURAL WORLD

The Earth was formed about 4500 million years ago. Today it is home to 1.3 million animal species, with perhaps millions more (mostly insects) as yet undiscovered. Our life-giving planet may be unique.

The Earth

First ban on CFCs

The hole in the ozone layer is caused mainly by Chlorofluorocarbons (CFCs), chemicals used in refrigerators and aerosol sprays. CFC gases released into the upper air stay around for many years, converting the ozone to oxygen.

Some countries have banned the use of CFCs in fridges and other products to protect the ozone layer from further damage.

First photochemical smog
Air pollution was a problem in the Middle Ages, when coal fires in London caused 'nuisance'. Photochemical smog involves the action of sunlight on chemicals in car exhaust gases and other pollutants. Los Angeles in California has suffered severe air pollution since the 1960s.

First volcanoes

More than 100 million years ago dinosaurs ran for shelter from erupting volcanoes. In fact there were volcanoes long before there were any animals. Rocks over 2500 million years old were formed by volcanoes.

First ozone loss

The first record of the 'hole' in the Earth's ozone layer was made in 1982 by scientists of the British Antarctic Survey. They discovered that some of the ozone in the atmosphere had disappeared.

First continents

Continents are the Earth's huge landmasses. About 200 million years ago there was one very large continent, which scientists call Pangaea. It split, first in two, and then into smaller pieces which drifted apart and gradually formed the continents as we know them today.

The supercontinent Pangaea

First rainforests

The primeval swamp-forests of 400 million years ago flourished in the Earth's warm, moist climate. But the prehistoric forest 'trees' were not conifers or flowering trees. They were giant ferns and club-mosses.

◁ A gibbon from the rain forest.

First ice age

The first ice ages happened about 2300 million years ago, in Pre-Cambrian times. The most recent ice age began about 1,600,000 years ago and ended 10,000 years ago.

First signs of global warming

The Earth has got cooler and warmer in cycles for millions of years. People began to add to the warming effect in the 1700s by burning fuels that release carbon dioxide and other gases. The term 'greenhouse effect' was first used in 1896.

Earth firsts

Biggest continent: Asia, 44 million km^2.

Biggest ocean: Pacific, 166 million km^2.

Longest river: Nile, 6695 km.

Oldest living things: Antarctic lichens and American creosote plant, both 10,000 years old.

First description of acid rain: in 1874.

Largest volcano: Mauna Loa on Hawaii.

First to reconstruct prehistoric animals: Georges Cuvier (1769–1852), using fossil bones.

First to know the Earth is round: The Greeks, by studying shadows of Earth and Moon during eclipses.

Animals

First animals with whiskers

Some animals of today use whiskers as extra sense-organs. The first whiskered land animals probably used them in the same way. These creatures were reptiles. A dog-like reptile called *Cynognathus* lived over 200 million years ago. It probably hunted like a dog, by sniffing and chasing.

◁ Archaeopteryx

First bird

The identity of the first bird is a mystery. Was it the crow-sized *Archaeopteryx* of 150 million years ago as most books say? Or was it *Protoavis texensis*, a chicken-sized animal with a long tail which lived 225 million years ago?

First monster crocodile

In 1991 South American scientists found the skull of a giant crocodile that lived eight million years ago. It was 12 metres long and weighed 12 tonnes and had 10-centimetre-long teeth. This Amazonian monster-crocodile would outweigh a modern elephant, and beats the dinosaur *Tyrannosaurus rex* to the title of the biggest carnivore that ever lived on land.

First tadpoles in space

Tadpoles hatched on the US Space Shuttle *Endeavour* in September 1992 were the first animals born in space, other than insects. Inside the orbiting spacecraft the weightless tadpoles performed gymnastics. They turned somersaults instead of wriggling as they swam.

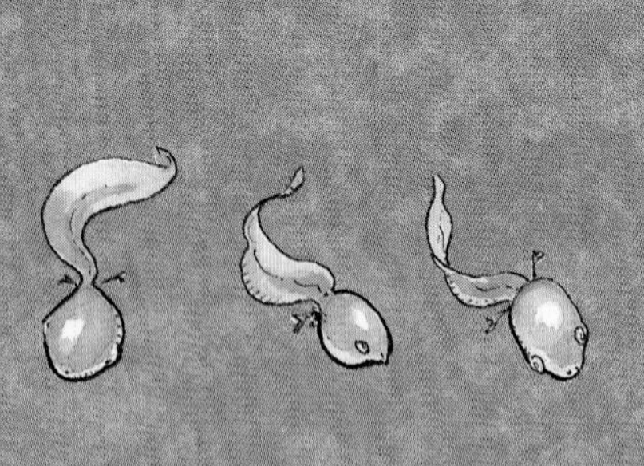

First horse

The first horse was the size of a cat and lived in dense forests about 50 million years ago. The first horse to look like a horse as we know it today was *Merychippus*, which lived about 15 million years ago. It was the size of a Shetland pony and could run swiftly over grassy plains on its single-toed hoofs.

First mass extinction by humans

The aurochs, a type of ox, and the dodo were killed off completely by the 1600s because they were overhunted. The American buffalo was almost wiped out by hunters between 1850 and 1880.

First amphibians

Amphibians were the first animals, apart from insects, to live on the land. They evolved about 400 million years ago from air-breathing fishes which had crawled out of the water. The first amphibian, *Ichthyostega*, looked like an outsize newt, and its descendents are today's frogs, toads and salamanders.

First sharks

The first sharks swam 400 million years ago. They were miniature versions of modern sharks, although some had strange spiny heads. Biggest among prehistoric sharks was *Carcharodon* (20 metres long), which lived 30 million years ago.

First known poisonous bird

The world's first poisonous bird was found in New Guinea in 1992. The Pitohui looks like a colourful starling, but it gives a nasty stomach ache to any snake or hawk that eats it.

Plants and People

First plants
The first plants to appear on Earth about 3000 million years ago were floating algae. By producing oxygen as they made food, plants altered the Earth's atmosphere. The planet became an environment fit for animals to evolve and flourish.

First conifers
Cone-bearing trees or conifers, were the first plants with seeds. They developed over 350 million years ago, and included cycads and ginkgoes, which survive to this day.

First land plants
Ferns were the first plants with roots and stems. Together with mosses, they grew in swamps about 400 million years ago.

First forests
Growing 350 million years ago in the first forests were giant ferns, clubmosses and horsetails which were much larger than their modern relatives. Some of these prehistoric plants had stems 30 metres tall. Their top branches could carry cones 75 centimetres long.

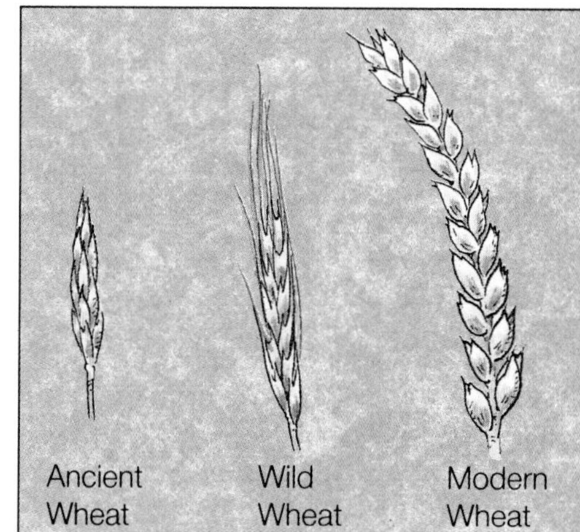

First domesticated cereal
Farmers first grew wheat in the valley of the Euphrates River (now in Iraq) about 9000 years ago. The first farmers harvested wild wheat, then learned to plant their own. Rye (8500 years ago) barley (7000 years ago) and rice (5000 years ago) were also grown in ancient times.

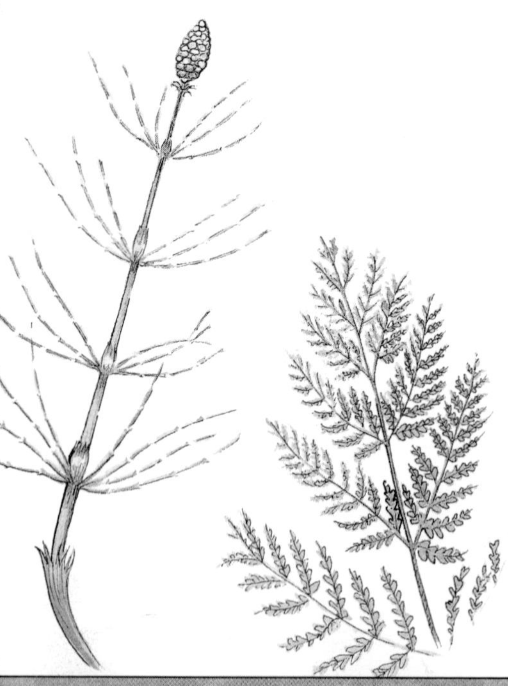

First flowering plants
Flowering plants were the last important group of plants to appear, about 150 million years ago. More than 250,000 species grow today, including flowering trees and shrubs. Flowering plants may have evolved from ferns. They did so well because their reproduction method gave them a great advantage over other types of plant.

One of the earliest flowering plants still surviving today is the magnolia.

First domesticated animals

It was at least 12,000 years ago that our Stone Age ancestors first tamed wild dog puppies. Sheep, goats and cattle were domesticated 10,000 years ago.

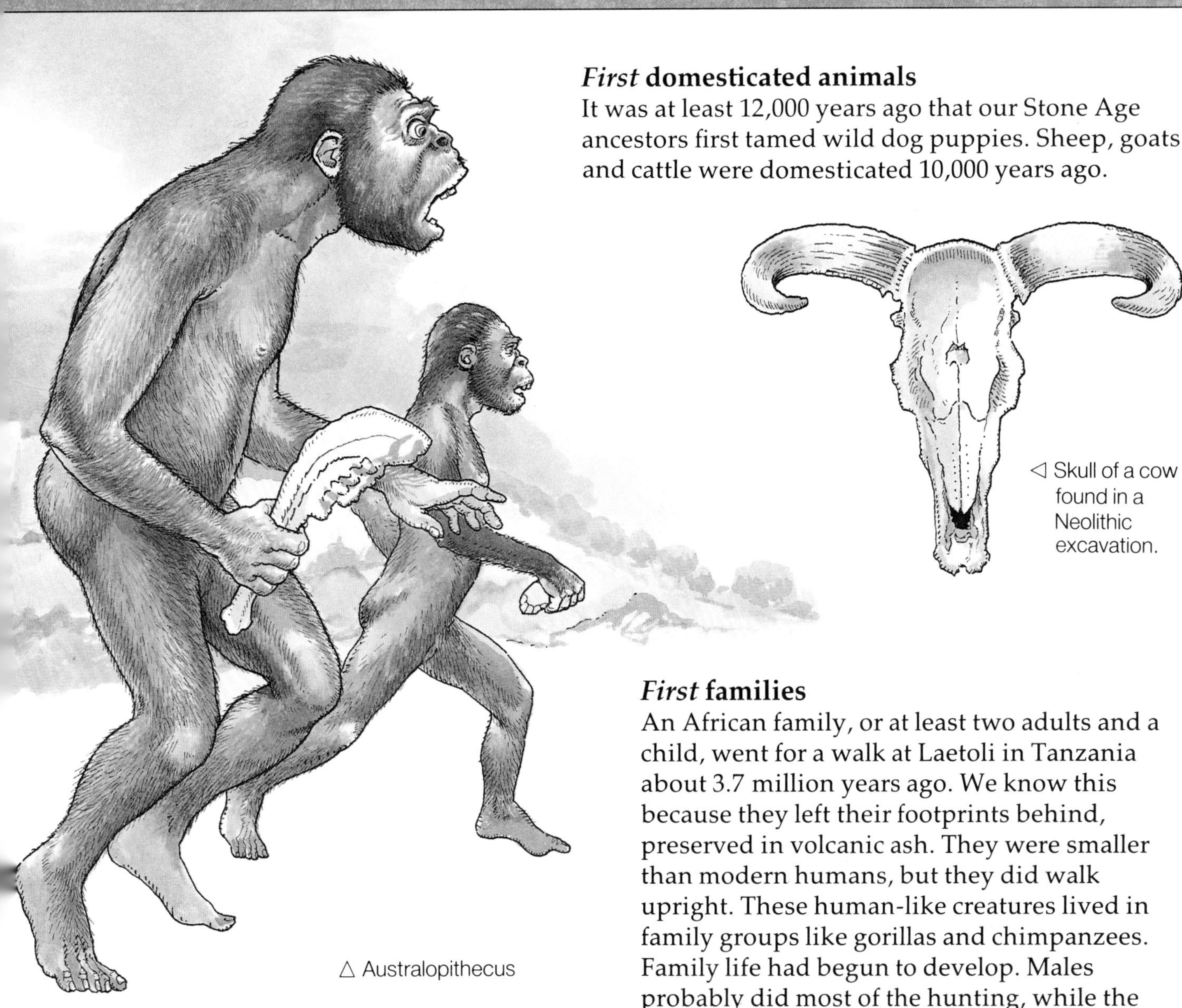

◁ Skull of a cow found in a Neolithic excavation.

△ Australopithecus

First families

An African family, or at least two adults and a child, went for a walk at Laetoli in Tanzania about 3.7 million years ago. We know this because they left their footprints behind, preserved in volcanic ash. They were smaller than modern humans, but they did walk upright. These human-like creatures lived in family groups like gorillas and chimpanzees. Family life had begun to develop. Males probably did most of the hunting, while the females and children foraged for food such as grubs, fruit and roots.

First human-like creatures

The first human-like creature was called *Australopithecus*. It lived more than 4 million years ago and walked on two legs. The first human was *Homo habilis* ('handy' or 'skilful man') and appeared about two million years ago. Humans with bigger brains developed from *Homo habilis*. Modern humans which looked and reasoned like us first lived 40,000 years ago. Scientists call our species *Homo sapiens sapiens* (wise, wise man).

First zoos

The first owner of a zoo was Queen Hatshepsut of Egypt, about 3500 years ago. Ancient Egyptians sent expeditions to East Africa to bring back monkeys, leopards, giraffes and other animals. Kings and emperors used to give lions or elephants as gifts to each other. The Roman emperor Augustus had 420 tigers and 260 lions, but just one hippopotamus and an equally lonely rhinoceros.

First theory of evolution

The idea of 'natural selection' was first put forward in the 1850s by Charles Darwin who noted that Galapagos Islands' tortoises evolved differently. He wrote a famous book called *The Origin of Species*, which was published in 1859.

TECHNOLOGY

The first technologists lived thousands of years ago in the Stone Age. They mastered the skills of fire-making and sewing animal skins into clothes. These were the first steps towards the space-age technologies of today.

Machines

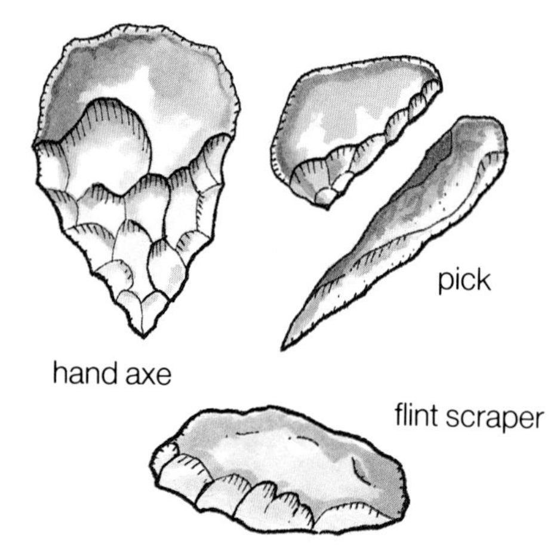

First tools

Over two million years ago in Africa, intelligent human-like creatures first picked up stones and sticks to use as tools. These creatures walked upright, so their hands were free to hold tools. Tool-making came about a million years after tool-using when more advanced humans learned how to chip stones into hammers, diggers, cutters and scrapers.

First irrigation

Farmers in dry lands found ways to water their crops over 4000 years ago. They dug ditches, and filled them with water, using machines such as the water-wheel and shadoof.

First metal tools

Our direct ancestors were Cro-Magnon people who lived about 40,000 years ago. They made tools of flint and bone, and used bows and arrows and the bowdrill (see right). The first metal tools were made from copper, which is soft and easily hammered, in about 8000 BC. By 3000 BC the metal-workers of Sumeria (now in Iraq) were using bronze, an alloy of copper and tin.

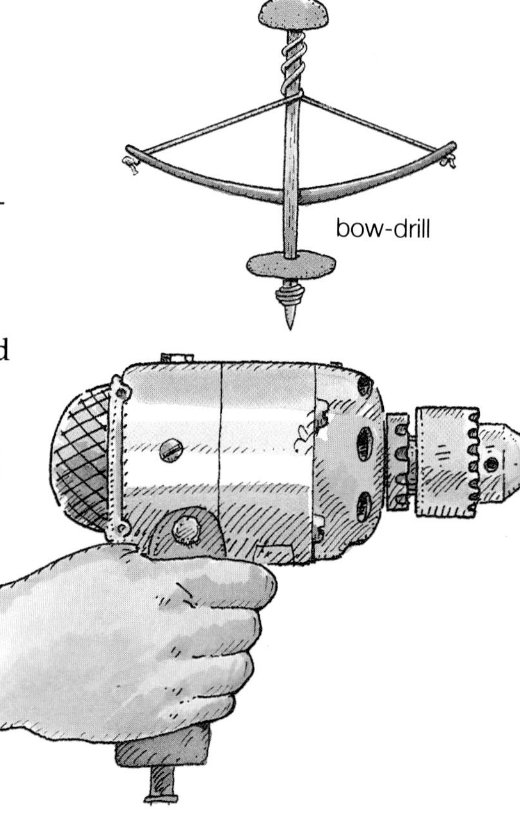

A modern electric drill. The first electric drill was invented in 1917. ▷

First potter's wheel
The secret of making pots from clay was discovered over 10,000 years ago. It was a key invention of early civilization. The potter's wheel came much later, first appearing in Mesopotamia about 5000 years ago. The pottery kiln fires pots and bricks, making them hard, and was invented at about the same time.

First **windmills**
Windmills first ground grain in the Middle East about AD 600. Their sails were set horizontally, like the blades of a cylinder lawnmower standing on end.

First **alarm clock**
Weight-driven mechanical clocks were invented in the 1200s. Their machinery could ring bells, and the first alarm clock was made in Germany in the 1360s.

▽ Alarm clock – 1960s style

First **wheelbarrow**
The Chinese had a good name for the wheelbarrow — they called it the 'wooden ox'. This simple handcart was in use in China by AD 200 and had a much bigger wheel than the modern wheelbarrow. It was just as useful as the ox too. The Chinese experimented with war barrows, armed with rockets, large passenger-carrying barrows and even wind-powered barrows fitted with a sail.

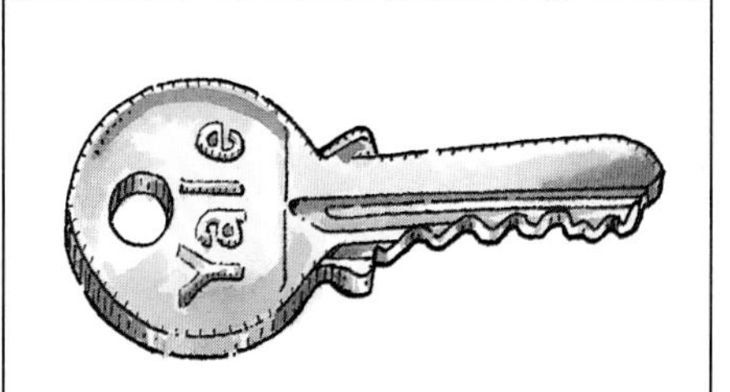

***First* Yale lock**
An American named Linus Yale patented a burglar-proof lock in 1861 which was described as 'magic' and 'infallible'. The Yale cylinder lock has remained as the same basic design ever since.

First **dynamo**
In 1831 the British scientist Michael Faraday showed that moving a magnet near a wire could produce an electric current. He had made the first dynamo, for generating electricity.

First **steam engines**
James Watt did not invent the steam engine. Thomas Savery (1698) and Thomas Newcomen (1712) made steam pumping engines for mines. These were the first real steam engines if the steam-toys of the Ancient Greeks are discounted. Watt's engine (1764) is so well known because it was powerful enough to drive factory machines and locomotives.

First **computer**
In 1823 the British mathematician and inventor Charles Babbage designed a steam-driven computer that was never built. It would have used punched-card programming. The first all-electronic digital computer was called ENIAC, built by the Americans J. P. Eckert and J. W. Mauchly in 1946. It weighed 30 tonnes, but had less power than a modern desktop machine.

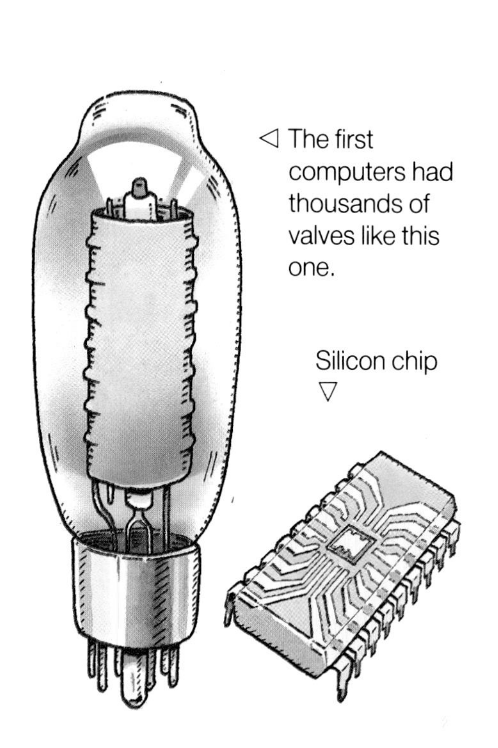

◁ The first computers had thousands of valves like this one.

Silicon chip ▽

Farming and Industry

First plough

Digging a field with a stick gave the first farmers backache. So they put handles on a large digging stick to make the first plough, which the farmer pushed, while his wife and children pulled. Metal blades and using oxen or horses soon made ploughing much faster. Wheeled ploughs allowed farmers to work heavy soils.

Aerial crop-spraying

Ancient Egyptian plough

First aerial crop-spraying

Fertilizers have been used since ancient times. Farming took to the air in 1921, with the first crop-spraying from aircraft. The planes flew slowly over the fields, their tanks filled with chemical plant foods or insecticides (to kill pests). Aerial crop-spraying can mean that the chemicals get blown onto neighbouring fields or gardens where they can kill plants and animals that cause no harm.

First translantic crops

No European had eaten potato, tomato, maize (sweetcorn), or chocolate before the 1500s. These foods were brought to Europe from America after the 'discovery' of the New World.

First moulting sheep

A sheep can now have an injection to make its wool fall off a month later. The technique is quicker than shearing, and was first demonstrated in Australia in 1991.

First horse collar

Between AD 800 and 900, the horse-collar appeared, together with iron horseshoes. The horse could now be put before the cart, with much greater power. Before this horses could not pull heavier carts, because the neck-harness then in use choked them.

Farming firsts

Growing wheat and raising cattle and sheep began in the Near and Middle East over 10,000 years ago.

Stone Age people in Papua New Guinea and elsewhere in Asia may have grown roots such as yams as early as 30,000 BC.

Farmers sowed seeds by hand until the mechanical seed drill was invented in England by Jethro Tull in 1701.

The threshing machine of 1834, and reaper-binder of 1873 heralded the arrival of the modern combine harvester.

First factory

Most manufactured goods were made by families working at home, until the 1700s. Spinners spun yarn and weavers wove cloth. In 1720, the first water-powered silk-spinning factory was opened in Derby, England.

1880s gas lamp

First gas lighting

William Murdock risked burning down his Cornish home in 1779 by lighting it with coal gas burning at the open end of an iron pipe. In 1807, a Manchester factory was lit with gas, and Pall Mall, a street in London, had the first city gas lamps. Gas was dominant until the 1880s when electric light became more popular.

First plastics

Celluloid was the first plastic, in 1870. One of its uses was to make film for the new snapshot cameras of the 1880s. In 1909, Bakelite became the first plastic made from synthetic resins (substances made from the chemicals in crude oil).

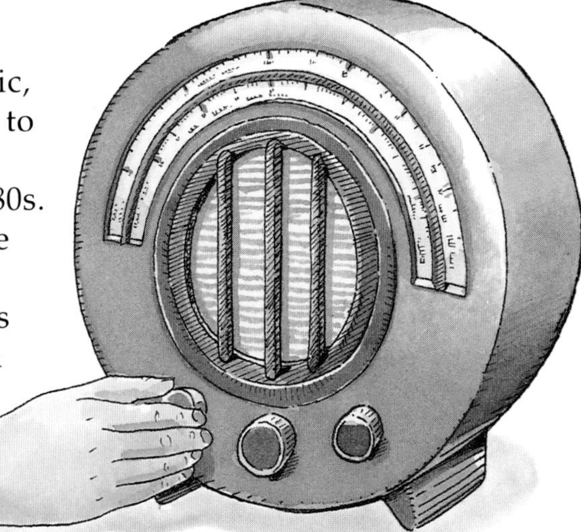

An early Bakelite radio ▷

First power station

The first power station began selling electricity in San Francisco, USA, in 1879. New York opened its first power station in 1882.

First jeans

The first pair of jeans were worn in 1874. They were cheap working trousers, made in the USA by Levi Strauss. The name 'jeans' has French and Italian origins, probably a reference to the Italian city of Genoa where cotton was imported from the Near East.

First oil well

Edwin Drake struck America's first oil in 1859, in Pennsylvania. The Chinese built the first drilling rigs 600 years earlier for salt and methane gas.

First nylon

Women first wore nylon stockings in 1940, just five years after an American chemist named Wallace H. Carothers had succeeded in making nylon. Nylon was the first synthetic fabric that could be ironed. It is still one of the most important man-made materials.

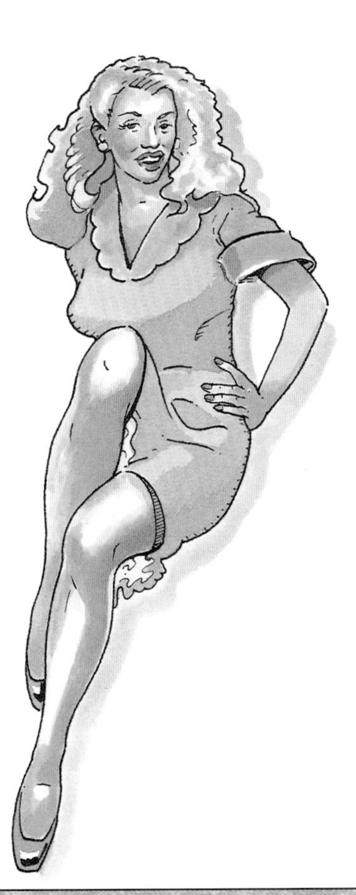

First robots

Skilled craftsmen of the Middle Ages made robot-like models called 'automata', to look like flying birds and dancing dolls. The first real robots worked in car factories in the 1970s.

Construction

First cement mixers

The Ancient Egyptians mixed cement 5000 years ago, but it stayed soft in water. Roman cement was made of slaked lime (lime mixed with water) and volcanic ash, which set even under water.

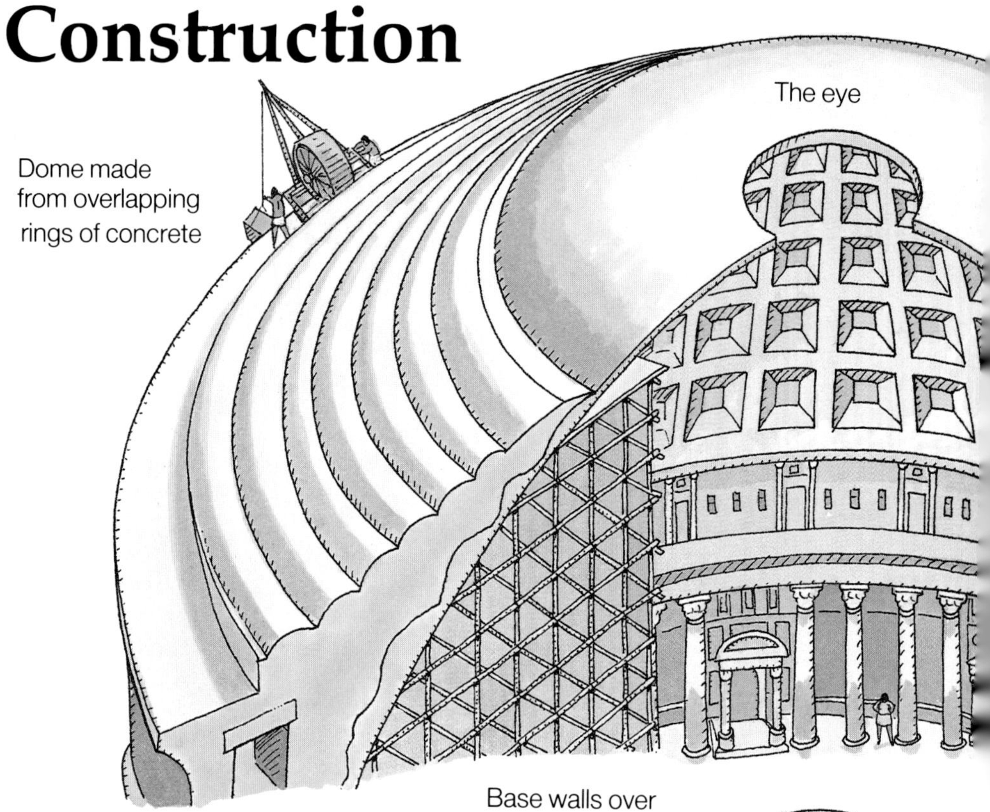

First building bricks

Builders in Mesopotamia (modern Iraq) and India made bricks 8000 years ago with their bare feet. They trod clay mixed with water and straw, packed the mixture into moulds and dried it in the sun. It was discovered later that oven-baked bricks were much harder, and needed no straw to resist cracking.

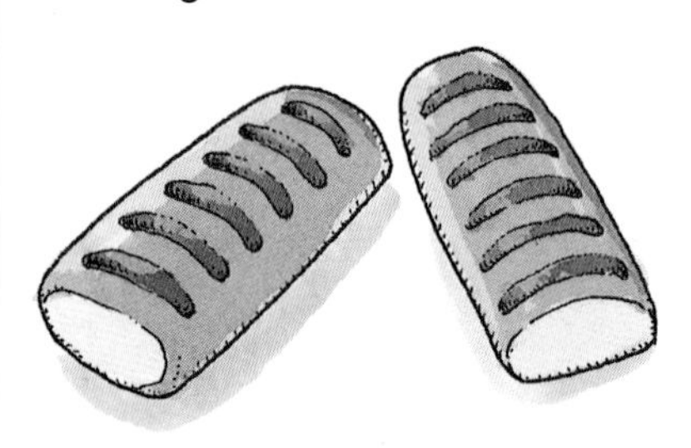

First dome

Engineers took the idea of the dome from beehive-shaped roofs on huts, such as those at Khirokitia in Cyprus dating from 5500 BC. The Romans perfected the dome in the Pantheon, a temple in Rome, which has a dome measuring 43 metres across.

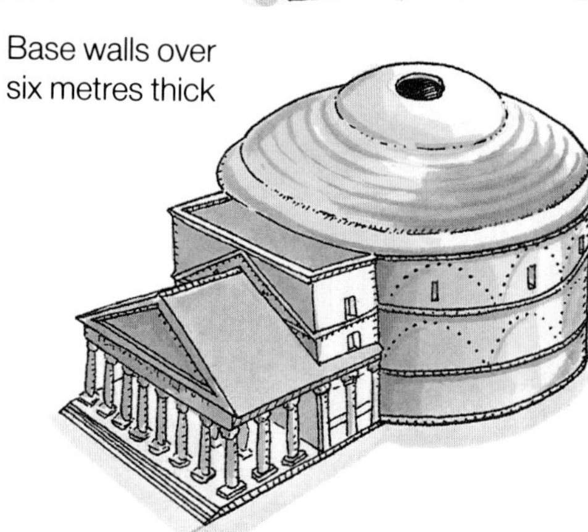

Construction Firsts

Reinforced concrete, strengthened with iron rods, was first tried in the 1860s. Pre-stressed concrete, in which steel rods are stretched before the concrete sets, came in the 1930s.

The first safety lift with an automatic brake was demonstrated in 1854 by its designer, Elisha Otis. Mr Otis stood on the lift and then calmly cut the lifting rope. To everyone's amazement (and relief) the lift did not plunge to the ground.

The first electric lifts were installed in the 1880s.

The first escalator was the brainchild of two American engineers George Wheeler and Jesse Reno, who designed a moving staircase in the 1890s. The first working escalator carried its passengers in a New York railway station in 1900.

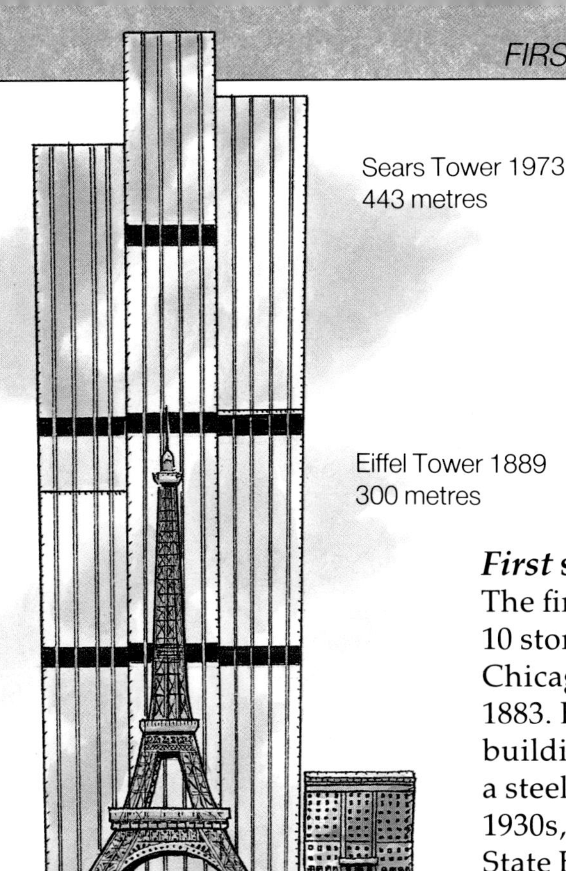

First motorways

Most roads were little better than dirt tracks before the 1900s. Tarred roads gave early motorists a smoother ride, then the Italians built the first motorway or autostrada in 1924. These express roads for cars bypassed towns, avoiding junctions and other hold-ups.

First skyscraper

The first 'skyscraper' was just 10 storeys high, built in Chicago by William Jenney in 1883. His new-style office building had walls hung from a steel-girder box. By the 1930s, New York's Empire State Building dwarfed even the Eiffel Tower of Paris. The tallest skyscraper is the Sears Tower in Chicago (110 storeys, 443 metres).

First giant glasshouse

Glasshouses for plants became popular in the 1700s. The biggest ever glasshouse was built in 1851 in London's Hyde Park for the Great Exhibition. Popularly known as the Crystal Palace, it was put together from 35,000 iron columns and girders. It was so big that thousands of people could stroll about inside.

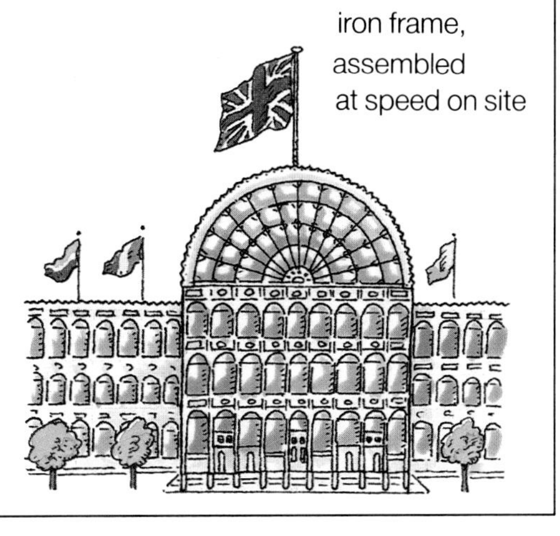

First tunnels

The first people to make both ends of a tunnel meet were the Romans, who drilled guide-holes to make sure they kept on course. The Assyrians diverted the River Euphrates in 2160 BC. In the dry river bed they dug a trench and built a brick tunnel in it. Then they let the river return to its original course.

First dam

People in the Middle East built earth dams to store water for irrigation 5000 years ago. Superdams came in the 1930s, with concrete arch dams such as the Hoover Dam in the USA, standing 221 metres high, and even bigger earth and rockfill dams.

Military

First weapons

Stone Age people may have settled quarrels peacefully, but since they used clubs, stones and spears to hunt animals, they probably picked them up to fight one another as well. Before 5000 BC missile-throwers, such as slingshots or bows, gave warriors a great advantage over opponents who had to move in close to swing a club.

First wind-up weapons

Heavy catapults and slingers were the first artillery weapons. They fired when taut cords, wound up by turning a handle, were released. Some of these 'war engines' fired giant arrows. Others hurled rocks to knock holes in walls, or blazing tar balls into an enemy stronghold. Some lobbed rotting corpses as ammunition.

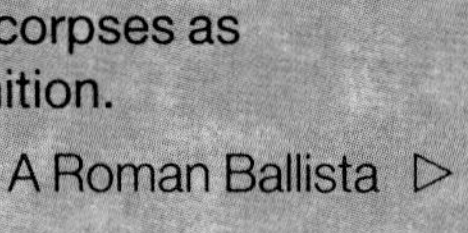

A Roman Ballista ▷

First rocket-fire

The Chinese scared away their enemies by inventing  gunpowder rockets, perhaps as early as AD 300. When bombarded by rocket-launchers firing arrows with exploding warheads, most invaders of China turned hurriedly for home.

First organized armies

Until about 3000 years ago, battles were skirmishes fought by bands of amateur soldiers. Then the Assyrians and Egyptians organized the first well-equipped armies and conquered large empires. Soldiers in chariots scattered enemy foot-soldiers by charging at them, firing arrows as they attacked.

First armour

Armour was worn thousands of years before medieval knights went to war clad in chain mail and plate armour. The Assyrians of 1000 BC wore armour of leather and bronze. Greeks and Romans wore bronze or steel armour, shaped to fit the chest, legs and head. Their shields gave extra protection against spears, arrows and swords.

First death ray

When the Romans attacked Sicily in 214 BC, the Greek scientist Archimedes set up a large mirror onto which the sun's rays were reflected from smaller, movable mirrors. The resulting beam of sunlight set fire to Roman ships at sea.

First machine gun
Early guns from the 1300s fired only one shot at a time. The Gatling gun of the American Civil War (1861-65) had ten barrels, rotated for rapid fire.

First tank
Tanks, originally a secret code name, first trundled into use during the First World War (1914-18). The British sent 32 tanks into action in 1916.

First atom bomb
The atomic bomb was made in secret during the Second World War. American planes dropped A-bombs on the cities of Hiroshima and Nagasaki in 1945, causing the Japanese to surrender.

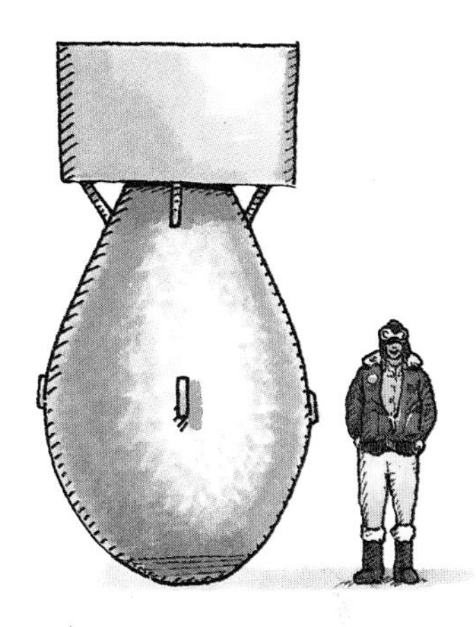

First battle between ironclads
Armoured warships fought for the first time in 1862, during the American Civil War. The South's ten-gun steamer *Merrimack* was challenged by the North's two-gun turret-ship *Monitor*. Neither ship suffered serious damage.

First nuclear submarine
A submarine that could cruise the Earth under water, without refuelling, slipped into the water in 1955. The US Navy's *Nautilus* had turbine engines driven with steam heated by a nuclear reactor.

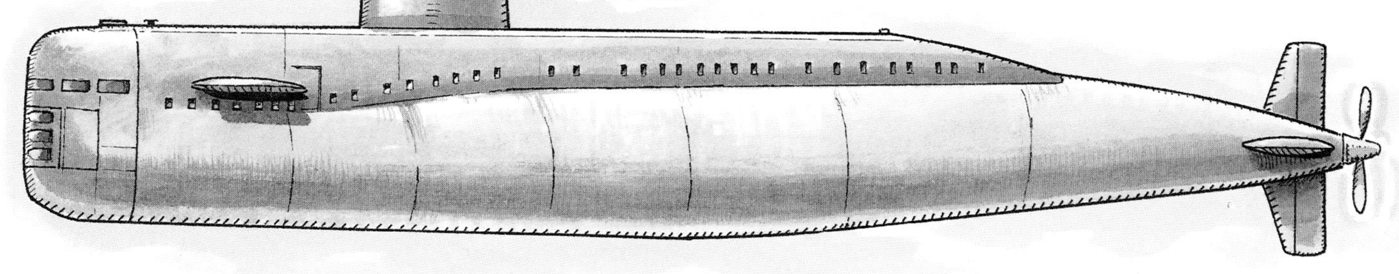

USS Nautilus

First aircraft carrier
The British navy first saw that aircraft could be useful at sea. They tried seaplanes, fitted with floats. Then in 1916 they converted HMS *Argos*, a half-finished passenger ship, into the first aircraft carrier. But before it was finished, a British pilot set down his Sopwith Pup biplane onto a flat deck fitted to the cruiser HMS *Furious*. It was the first landing on a ship's deck.

First 'invisible' bomber
Most planes make a big 'blip' on a radar screen, but not the US Air Force's F-117A Stealth fighter-bomber. Almost invisible to radar, its batwing shape and secret 'muffling' devices let it fly undetected to its target.

F117A Stealth plane

FIRST ROCKET-FIRE.
FIRST MACHINE GUN
FIRST DEATH RAY

TRANSPORT

Since the 1700s, people have had the means to move themselves and their goods further and faster. Transport firsts have revolutionized the way we move over land, across and beneath the oceans and into the air.

Land

First cartwheels

The first wheels were made 5000 years ago, by fixing pieces of wood together. The first carts had two big solid wheels.

First saddles and stirrups

Clay models found in India show that people were sitting on saddles to ride horses by 2500 BC. Stirrups came later, in the AD 500s, and helped riders charging into battle to keep in their seats.

First steam carriage

The Frenchman Nicolas Cugnot crashed the world's first steam carriage in 1769.

First railway

The first public, steam railway opened in England in 1825. The first train along its Stockton to Darlington line had 33 carriages.

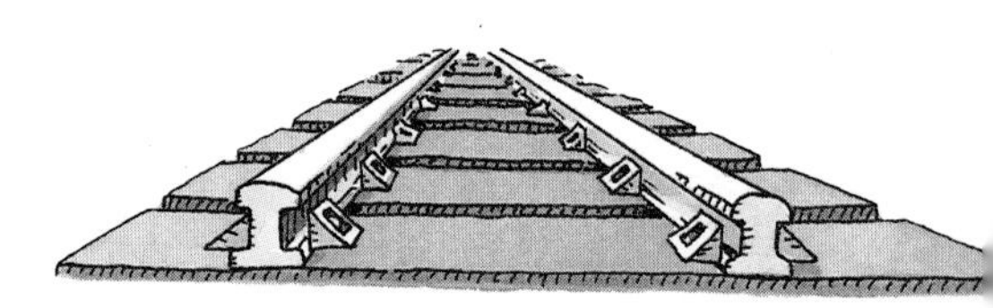

First bicycles

Energetic people in the early 1800s dashed about on dandy-horses. These first bicycles had no pedals. A rider's feet did all the work. The first modern-looking bicycle was Pierre Michaux's vélocipede of 1861.

The 1870s ordinary bicycle, the penny-farthing, was a racer. In its day, it was as hi-tech as the modern Olympic sprint bike with its carbon fibre body is now.

First (and last) 'Wogglebug'

In 1907, a Stanley steam car, nicknamed 'Wogglebug', reached 241 kilometres per hour.

Land Transport Firsts

The first Pony Express rider galloped away on 3 April 1860. This famous Missouri-to-California mail service lasted only 18 months before being replaced by the telegraph system.

The first self-propelled land vehicles had sails. The Dutch, a nation of great sailors, experimented with sailing carts around 1600.

First car
Karl Benz built the first car (and its engine) in Germany in 1885. On his first trip he hit a wall, but soon learned to drive.

First blown-up tyre
An air-filled (or pneumatic) tyre was invented in the 1880s and used in the first cars.

First steam train to travel at 200 kilometres per hour
In July 1938 the British locomotive *Mallard* hauled a seven-coach train weighing 245 tonnes at almost 203 kilometres per hour.

First electric train
In 1879, 30 people enjoyed a ride behind Werner Von Siemens's electric mini-train, the first electric train ever demonstrated. A Siemens–Halske electric train held the world speed record of 210 kilometres per hour by 1903.

First electric wipers
Early car drivers wore goggles because the vehicles had no windscreens. When screens were fitted, drivers had to wipe away rain and oil with a cloth. In 1916, the first cars with automatic wipers went on sale.

First underground railway
The world's first under-street railway opened in London in 1863. It had steam locomotives, and tunnels full of smoke.

First supertrains
Japanese 'Bullet' trains started the supertrain era in the 1960s when they began regular services at speeds of 200 kilometres per hour.

◁ The *Blue Flame*

The first mass-produced car was Ford's Model T, built from 1908 to 1927. Ford offered it in any colour as long as it was black!

The first traffic lights halted cars in Detroit, USA in 1919.

The 1960s bubble cars were cheap, tiny, and easy to park. The passenger seat was behind the driver and the door was at the front.

First car to travel at 1000 kilometres per hour
In 1970 a rocket car, *The Blue Flame* driven by Gary Gabelich of the USA, set a land speed record of 1016 kilometres per hour. The current record is 1019 kilometres per hour, set by Richard Noble in the jet-engined *Thrust 2* in 1983.

Water

First sailing craft

The first water voyagers to hoist a sail were Egyptians, about 5000 years ago. Before that, people used paddles to push boats along.

First sea voyages

The Phoenicians sailed all around the Mediterranean (1000 to 500 BC). They voyaged into the Atlantic, north to Britain and south along the shores of Africa.

First ship with paddles, screws and sails

In 1858 the *Great Eastern* was the biggest ship afloat at 19,000 tonnes and 211 metres long. Designed by Isambard Kingdom Brunel, it was the only ship ever built with paddlewheels and screws, as well as six masts of sails.

First rudder

The stern rudder was a Chinese invention, copied by Arab and European shipbuilders in the 1200s. The rudder was moved by a tiller. Earlier craft were steered by a large stern oar, like those on Viking ships.

First steamship

In 1783, in France the Marquis Jouffroy d'Abbans showed off the first paddle-steamer. John Fitch's curious 12-paddle steamboat carried 30 people along the Delaware River four years later.

Fitch's steamboat

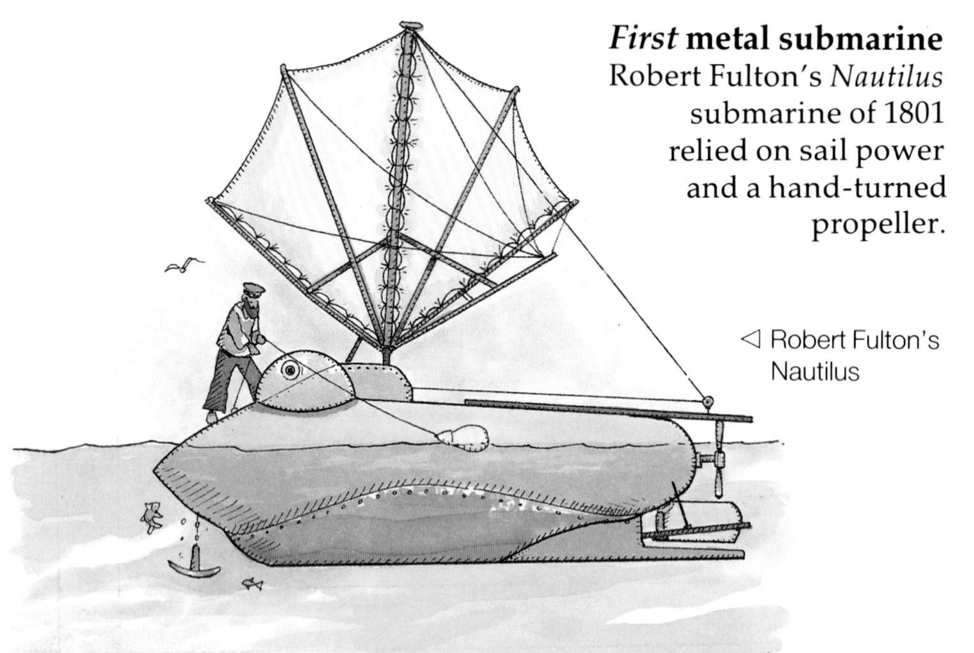

◁ Robert Fulton's Nautilus

First metal submarine

Robert Fulton's *Nautilus* submarine of 1801 relied on sail power and a hand-turned propeller.

First compass

The magnetic compass was first used by Chinese travellers. It reached the West in the 1100s. By 1300, the compass was marked with 32 points of direction to aid navigation.

First clipper ships

The first clippers were built in the 1840s. They carried tea from China and gold diggers to California. A clipper could cross the Atlantic in 12 days and sail from England to Australia in 60 days.

Water Transport Firsts
The first steam-powered warship was the *Demologos*, designed by the American Robert Fulton in 1814. Seven years earlier, Fulton's *Clermont* began the world's first regular steamboat service, along the Hudson River.

The first purpose-built lifeboat, aptly named the *Original*, was built by Henry Greathead of South Shields, England, in 1790.

The *Titanic* was the largest ship in the world when it sank on its maiden voyage in 1912.

Admirals worried about steam battleships running out of coal. Not until 1871 did the British navy risk sending to sea a battleship with no sails. This was HMS *Devastation*.

The *Great Eastern* ▽

First successful female Channel swimmer

The American Gertrude Ederle was 19 years old when she swam from France to England on 6 August 1926. Her time of 14 hours 39 minutes set a new record.

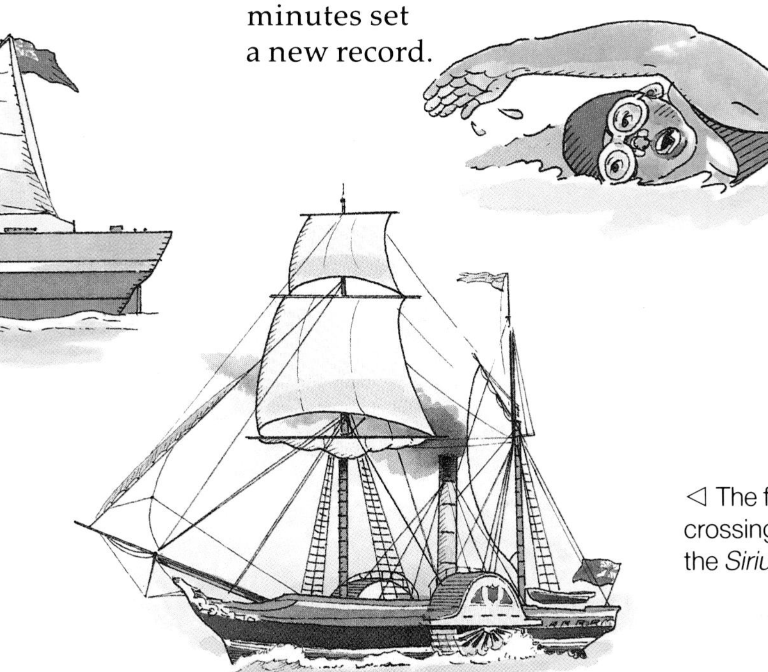

◁ The first Atlantic-crossing steamer – the *Sirius*

First steamer to cross the Atlantic Ocean

In 1838, the *Sirius* became the first ship to cross the Atlantic under steam power alone, narrowly beating the *Great Western*. The steamer *Savannah* had crossed the Atlantic in 1819, but used sails most of the way.

First magnet-powered ship

An electro-magnetic craft was launched in 1992 in Japan. It works by sending an electric current through a magnetic field. The resulting force sends a jet of water shooting out at high speed, and the craft races forwards. Future magnetic ships should be quiet, fast and energy-efficient.

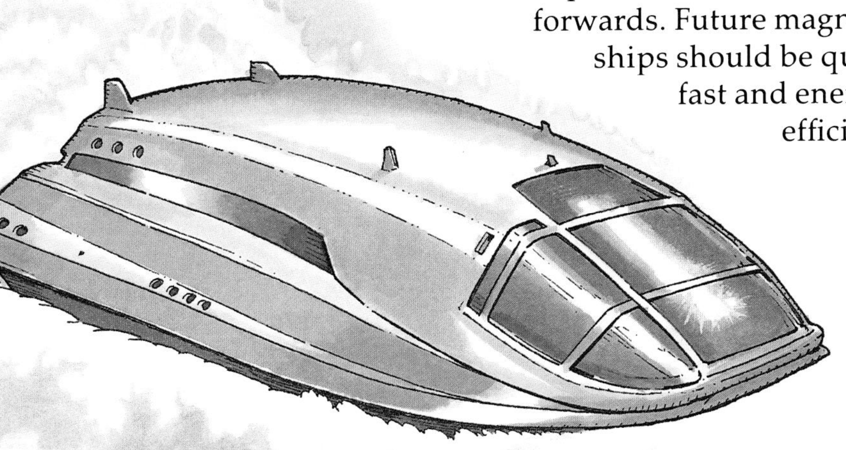

First oil tanker

The first oil tankers, such as the *Vaderland* (1872), carried a dangerous mixture of oil and passengers. The *Gluckauf* (1886) was much safer. Like a modern tanker, it had engines at the stern and separate tanks for its oil cargo.

First hovercraft

Christopher Cockerell was the British inventor who fixed two tins to a hairdryer to test his theory that an 'air-cushion vehicle' would work. The world's first hovercraft was the SRN1, built in 1959. The first passengers made hover-flights across the English Channel in 1966.

Air

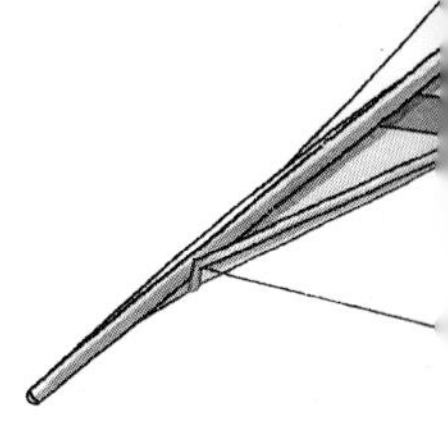

First hot-air balloonists

Etienne and Joseph Montgolfier's hot-air balloon carried the first balloonists over Paris on 21 November 1783. Pilâtre de Rozier and the Marquis d'Arlandes were in its basket.

First powered aircraft flight

Orville Wright flew for 12 seconds on the morning of 17 December 1903. He went 36.5 metres in the *Flyer*, the plane he had built with his brother Wilbur. They also built its petrol engine.

First woman to fly solo from England to Australia

A year after Amy Johnson learned to fly in 1929, she set off from England to Australia, in her tiny Tiger Moth biplane. She landed in Darwin nearly three weeks later, on 24 May 1930. This feat made Amy Johnson one of the 1930s flying stars. She died in a flying accident in 1941.

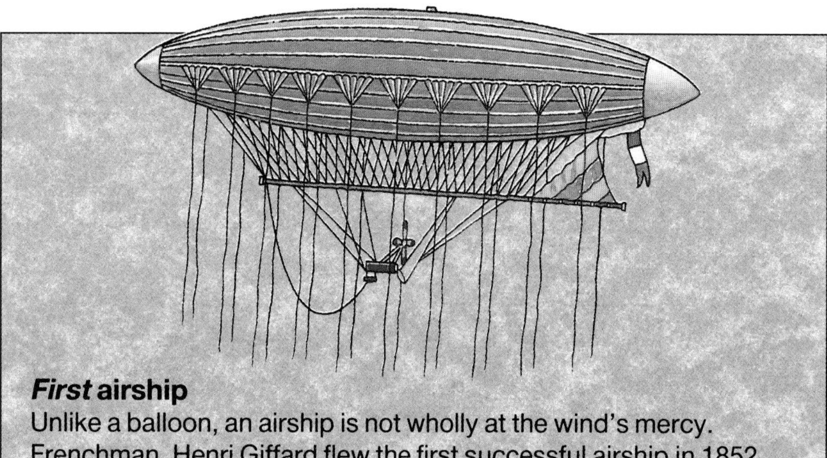

First airship

Unlike a balloon, an airship is not wholly at the wind's mercy. Frenchman, Henri Giffard flew the first successful airship in 1852. Hanging under its gasbag was a steam engine driving a propeller. Its first trial flight took Giffard 27 kilometres in 3½ hours. Alberto Santos-Dumont of Brazil flew the first petrol-engined airship in 1898.

Gossamer Albatross

First cross-Channel flights by pedal-power

In 1979, Bryan Allen pedalled *Gossamer Albatross* across the Channel in 8 hours 40 minutes.

First non-stop global flight

A US Air Force B-50 first flew non-stop round the world in 1949, refuelling in flight. The first global flight without mid-air refuelling was in 1986. Squeezed inside the light propeller-driven *Voyager*, Jeana Yeager and Dick Rutan flew around the world in just over nine days.

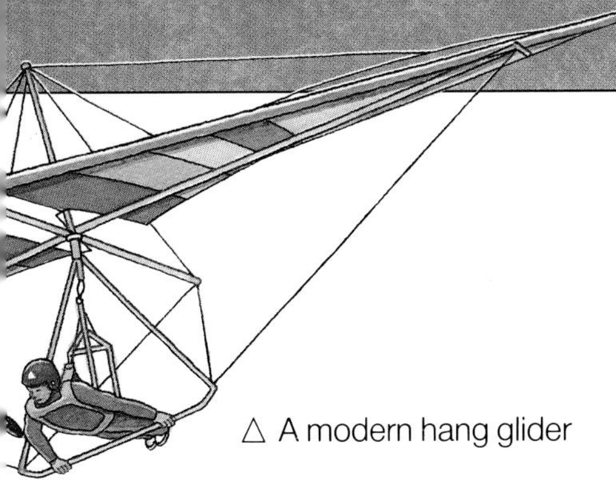

△ A modern hang glider

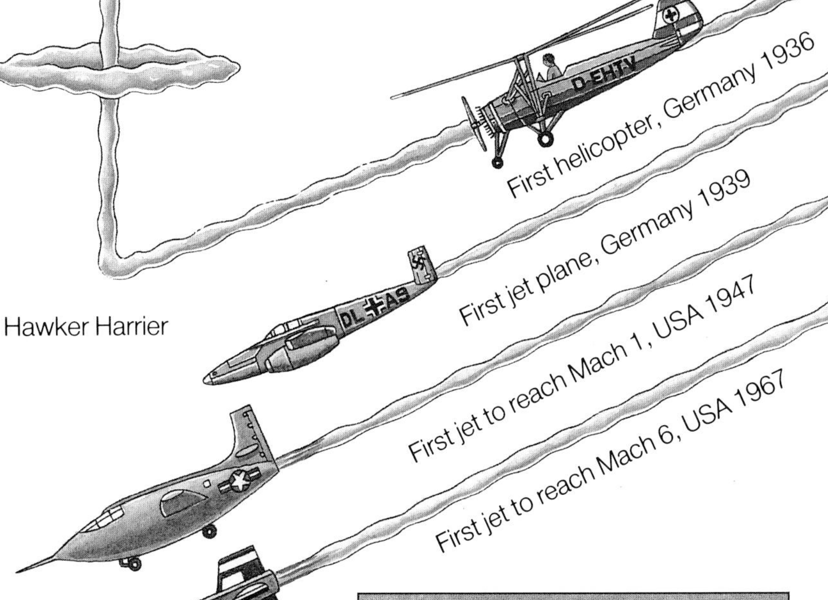

First hang glider

The German, Otto Lilienthal leapt off hillsides to test his hang glider. He made glides of up to 250 metres, but was killed in 1886 when he crashed to Earth.

First to bale out and live

In 1808, Jordarki Kuparanto jumped out of his balloon when it caught fire. He was the first flier to save his life by using a parachute.

First flying doctor

The first flying doctor, K. St Vincent Welch, took to the air in Queensland, Australia on 15 May 1928 and treated 255 isolated patients in the first year. John Flynn (a missionary) and Alfred Traeger (a radio engineer) started Australia's Flying Doctor service.

Flight Firsts

First solo flight across the Atlantic: Charles Lindbergh in *Spirit of St Louis* (1927).

First solo round the world flight: Wiley Post (1933).

First jet airliner: de Havilland Comet (1952).

First test flight of Boeing 747 and *Concorde*: (1969).

First balloon to fly the Atlantic: *Double Eagle* II (1978).

First trans-Atlantic hot-air balloon: *Virgin Atlantic Flyer* (1987).

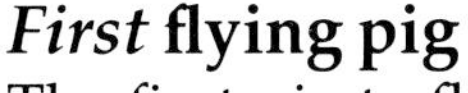

First flying pig

The first pig to fly was British! It took off with the pioneer pilot J. T. C. Moore-Brabazon in 1909. The piglet passenger's mission proved that 'pigs might fly' after all!

First tailless helicopter

The Russian Ka-50 Werewolf has no tail rotor, but two main rotors, one above the other. If its tail falls off, it still flies. Other helicopters would twirl to earth.

First swing-wing plane

The swing-wing Bell X5 was based on a wartime German design. Only two were made in 1951, and one crashed. The first swing-wing warplane was the F-111A, first built in 1964.

SCIENCE AND INVENTION

The first scientists lived thousands of years ago. They were astronomers, mathematicians and inventors. One of the oldest sciences is medicine, which in the early days was often mixed up with magic and superstition.

Medicine

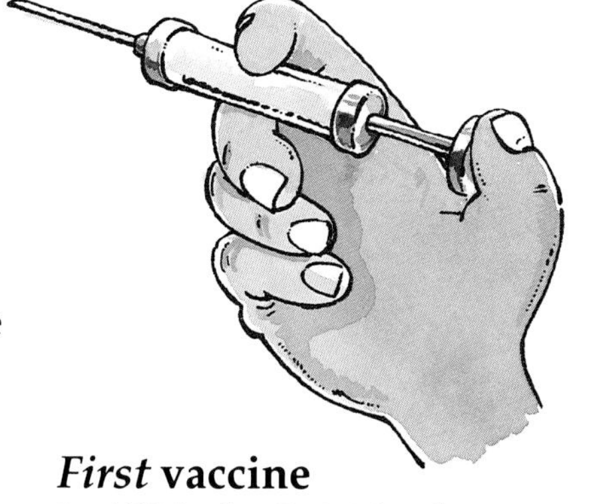

First doctors

The first doctors used medicines made from plants. They also performed surgery, even on the skull. The Chinese used acupuncture (needle-treatment) 3000 years ago. Ancient Indian surgeons operated on eyes and stomachs.

First vaccine

In 1796, the British physician Edward Jenner vaccinated a boy against smallpox by an injection of cowpox, a milder form of the illness.

First throne with built-in hearing aid

In 1819, deaf King John VI of Portugal owned a speaking chair. Courtiers shouted into lions' mouths in its hollow arms, and the sounds went through the chair to his ears.

First anatomists

The first doctors had little idea what went on inside the body. The Greeks cut open dead bodies to find out more, and in the 1500s anatomists examined the human body in detail for the first time.

Vesalius (1514–64) made careful drawings of the human anatomy.

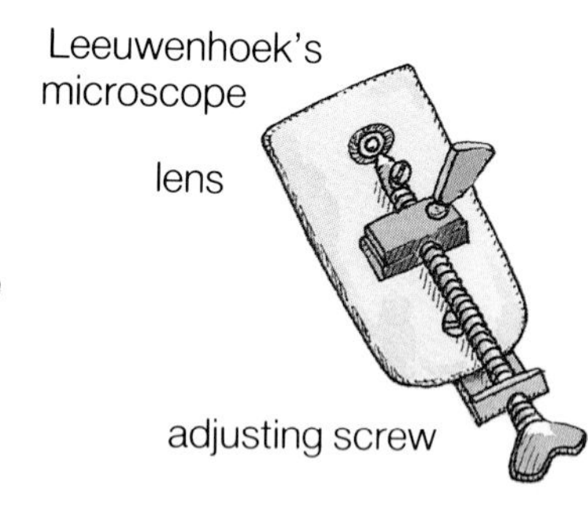

First person to see bacteria

In 1683, Dutch scientist Anton van Leeuwenhoek was startled to see living things much tinier than insects in a dish of pond water. He was the first to see bacteria.

First person to show how blood flows in the body

Early anatomists guessed that the heart, lungs and blood must be connected in some way. But doctors were not sure how until William Harvey published a book in 1628. In this book, Britain's royal physician showed that the heart pumps blood around the body.

First mad-dog-bite treatment

In 1885, Louis Pasteur saved the life of a nine-year-old boy bitten by a dog with rabies. Rabies had no known cure, so doctors were sure the boy would die. But Pasteur inoculated the boy, Joseph Meister, with a vaccine he had made from weak rabies virus. It worked, and the boy lived.

First germ-killing spray

In 1865, surgeon Joseph Lister used a steam kettle to spray carbolic acid into the air of his operating theatre. He rightly suspected that by killing germs, he could prevent infections.

First to discover X-rays

The German physicist Wilhelm Roentgen discovered X-rays accidentally in 1895. While experimenting with a cathode ray tube, he saw crystals in the room glowing. The crystals glowed even when he moved them next door. Rays from the tube had passed through brick walls to hit them! Roentgen named the mystery rays X-rays. They gave doctors their first pictures of people's insides.

First anaesthetics

An American, Crawford Long used ether to make patients unconscious during surgery in 1842.

First germ-killer mould

A mould in a dish was the key to making the first antibiotic, penicillin. Alexander Fleming discovered the mould in 1928. It had killed germs around it. Doctors used penicillin to combat infection from 1941 onwards.

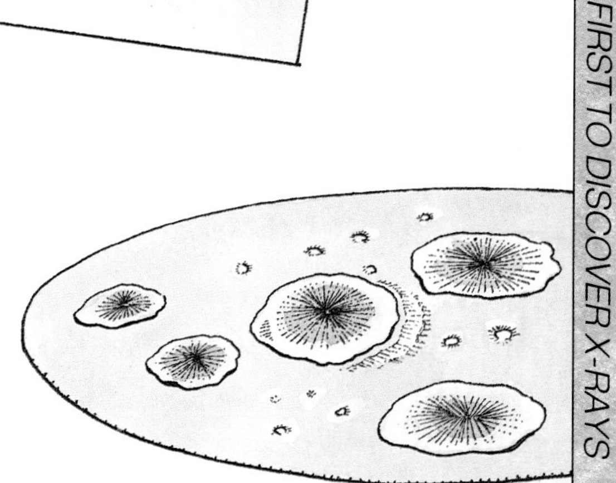

Mould of penicillium grown on a culture

Medical Firsts

- 700BC First false teeth.
- 1790 First mechanized dental drill.
- 1816 First stethoscope
- 1851 First ophthalmoscope for examining the eye.
- 1863 Pasteurization, to kill germs.
- 1866 Gregor Mendel works out laws of heredity, using peas.
- 1899 First aspirin, for pain relief.
- 1897 First surgical repairs to a beating heart.
- 1898 First proof that mosquitoes carry malaria.
- 1901 First identification of human blood groups.
- 1929 First iron lung machine.
- 1944 First kidney machine.
- 1954 First polio vaccine.

First heart transplant

In 1967, South African surgeon Christiaan Barnard took out the diseased heart of a sick patient and replaced it with a healthy heart taken from a dead person. Heart, liver and kidney transplants are now done with success.

Science Discoveries

First iron smelting

From about 1200 BC people wanted to use iron, rather than bronze. Iron was harder and stronger. The Chinese developed efficient bellows to blow air into a furnace, and led the world in the smelting of iron.

Ancient Greek clepsydra or water clock. The name meant 'water-thief'.

First laws of motion

Newton's three laws of motion, published in 1687, became the basis for modern physics. They explain the movements of all objects and the forces which act on them, in space and on the Earth. An apple may not have hit his head, but watching falling objects must have helped Newton discover gravity.

First clocks

Time-keepers in the ancient world included slow-burning sticks or ropes, water clocks and sun-dials or shadow-clocks. The Romans even had pocket sun-dials. Hour-glasses filled with sand came later, in the AD 700s.

First mathematicians

Ancient Egyptian and Babylonian scholars worked out calendars and developed ways of counting and measuring about 5000 years ago. They often based measuring units on various parts of the body such as fingers, palms, arms and feet.

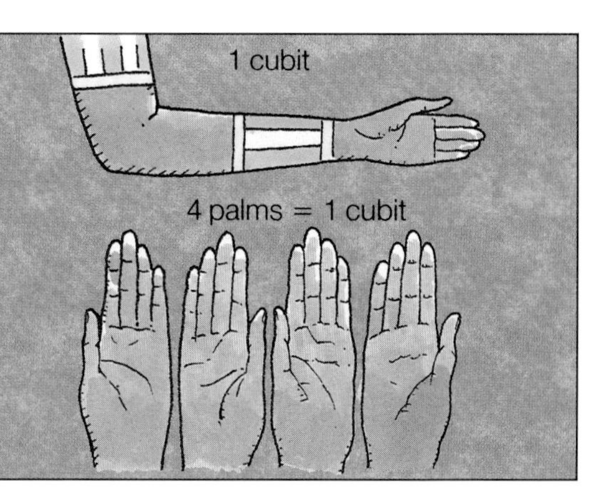

First electrical shocks

In the 1600s, people actually enjoyed getting an electric shock by touching a friction machine—a ball of sulphur electrically charged when spun rapidly.

First astronomers

Star-gazing 3000 years ago was connected with religion and astrology. This was the belief that the heavens guided events on Earth. The Chinese and Babylonians named stars, charted their positions, and recorded eclipses of the Sun and Moon.

The Universe according to the early astronomer Ptolemy, who believed the Earth was at the centre of the solar system.

First finders of oxygen

Two scientists discovered oxygen at about the same time in different countries. These people were Karl Scheele in Sweden and Joseph Priestley in Britain. They announced their discoveries in 1774, but the name 'oxygen' was the inspiration of the French chemist, Lavoisier.

A modern dry battery.

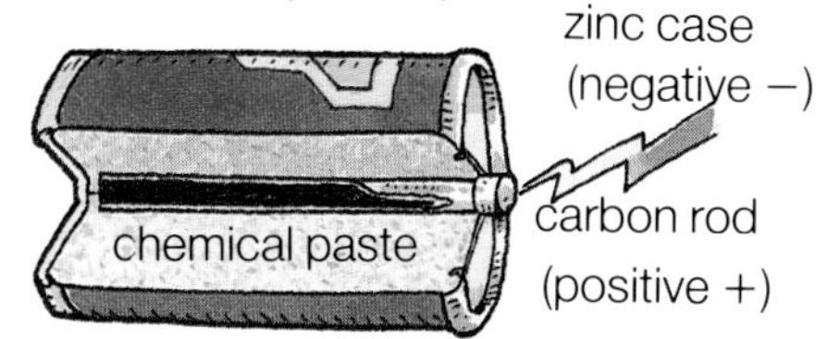

First battery

Alessandro Volta made the first battery in 1799. It was a pile of zinc and copper discs, separated by paper moistened with acid or salt water.

First transistor

The transistor was invented in 1948. Small, hard to break and using less power than the old fashioned valve, it provided the means to miniaturize radios and other electronic goods.

First artificial satellite

The Soviet Union launched the first artificial satellite into orbit on 4 October 1957. *Sputnik 1* was small, weighing just over 83 kilograms, but its radio 'bleeps' sent a clear signal around the world that the Space Age had begun.

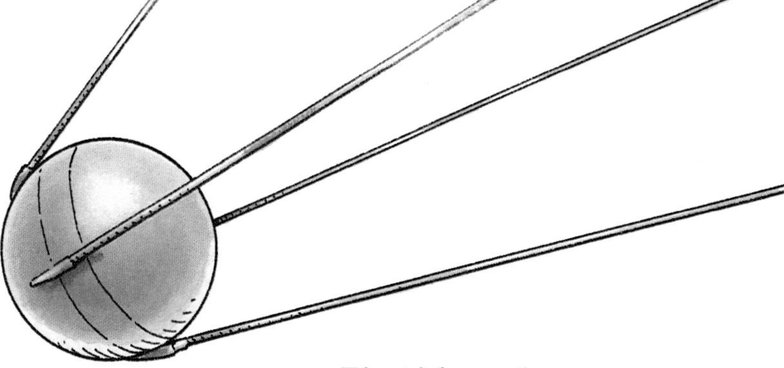

First to discovery radium

Working in a shed, Marie Curie and her husband Pierre discovered the radioactive elements radium and polonium in 1898.

First ideas about atoms

About 400 BC, the Ancient Greeks decided that everything was made of tiny atoms. 'Atom' is Greek for 'uncuttable'.

A 1940s valve radio was too heavy to carry around, unlike the 1950s transistor radio.

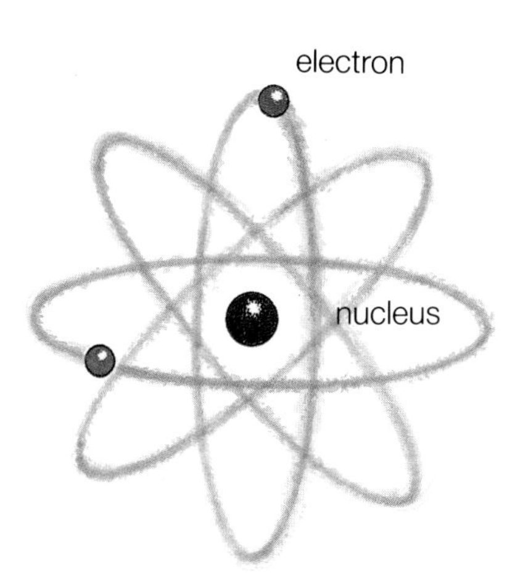

First photo of a molecule

Molecules are made of atoms joined together, but are still incredibly tiny. The first photo of a molecule was taken in 1988. It showed a protein molecule, about one millionth of a centimetre across, found in peas. The 'camera' was a scanning tunnelling microscope. This device and its partner, the atomic force microscope, can see details as small as an atom!

First photo of a molecule ▷

First chromosome code-crackers

Francis Crick and James Watson discovered the structure of DNA in 1953. All livings things are made up of cells. Cells contain chromosomes made of a chemical called DNA. Each DNA molecule looks like a twisted ladder or double helix, and is a codebook of inherited characteristics, containing coded instructions or genes.

Communications

First books
The first books were written by hand. Before paper was invented in about 50 BC, 'pages' were made of tablets of clay or wood. Books were also written on lengths of papyrus or parchment. To read the book, you unrolled the scroll.

First printing
The first book printed on a screw-press was the Gutenberg Bible in 1454. Johannes Gutenberg, from Germany, made Europe's first printing presses with movable type, although metal letters were also used to print books in China and Korea in the 11th century.

First snap-shot camera
The first cameras in the 1840s were large and heavy, and formed their pictures on wet metal plates. Dry celluloid film was invented in 1884. Four years later Eastman–Kodak began selling the first handy-sized box cameras.

From the 1880s people could carry a camera everywhere, taking snapshots for the photo album.

First typewriter
Until the 1800s, people wrote only with pens and pencils. The first typewriter that worked was designed in 1867 in America by Christopher Scholes, with Carlos Glidden and Samuel Soulé. Electric typewriters were invented in the 1920s.

The keyboard layout (beginning QWERTY) was meant to stop too-fast typing from tangling the keys.

First stamps
There were letter-carrying services before postage stamps. The first stamps to have glue on their backs were licked on 1 May 1840. They cost a penny, bore a picture of Queen Victoria of Great Britain, and had to be cut out with scissors. A retired British schoolteacher called Rowland Hill thought up the idea.

***First* record**
In 1877 (the year after Bell first used the phone) Thomas Alva Edison recorded the first words on his phonograph — a foil-covered cylinder. They were 'Mary had a little lamb'. Edison rewound the cylinder and, as a needle traced the grooves in the foil, heard his own voice. He had made the first record. Flat disc records came in 1887, with Emile Berliner's gramophone.

The phonograph horn amplified the sounds.

***First* criminal caught by radio**
In July 1910, urgent radio signals flashed from the liner *Montrose* steaming from London to Quebec. A suspicious couple were aboard. A detective steamed in pursuit across the Atlantic and arrested the murderer Dr Crippen and his accomplice Ethel le Neve.

***First* radio signals**
James Clerk Maxwell and Heinrich Hertz researched the theory of radio waves in the 1800s. The first dramatic demonstration of 'wireless' came in 1901 when Guglielmo Marconi sent a Morse code message across the Atlantic.

***First* television service**
John Logie Baird demonstrated television in 1926. But a rival electronic system was preferred for the first television service, started by the BBC in 1936.

***First* by satellite**
The Telstar satellite relayed the first television pictures 'live' across the Atlantic in 1962.

***First* colour television**
Television pictures were in black and white until the 1950s, although Baird had experimented with colour in 1928. America began colour television transmissions in 1953. Other countries switched to colour in the 1960s. Today three systems for colour television are used worldwide.

***First* 'phone call**
In 1876 Alexander Graham Bell used his new telephone to call for his assistant.

A modern hand-held mini-television. The first television sets had 18-centimetre screens.

HISTORY

In ancient times, every major civilization (Egyptian, Chinese, Indian, Greek, Roman) had its historians. From their writings and from crumbling ruins of vanished cities, we get glimpses of their long-lost worlds.

Ancient World

First major empire

Sargon of Akkad built the first great empire in the 2300s BC, based in Mesopotamia.

First construction to kill a million people

Building the 2400-kilometre-long Great Wall of China was more than just hard work. Folksong and legend claim that a million Chinese workers (mostly slaves) died building it. China's first emperor, Shih Huangdi, ordered the joining up of three older walls in 214 BC, to make a barrier between his empire and the fierce Mongol raiders of the steppes.

First towns and cities

The oldest known town is Jericho, near the Dead Sea, where people have lived for almost 10,000 years. Cities grew from villages. Some of the earliest were in Sumer (now in Iraq) around 3500 BC, in the Tigris–Euphrates river valley.

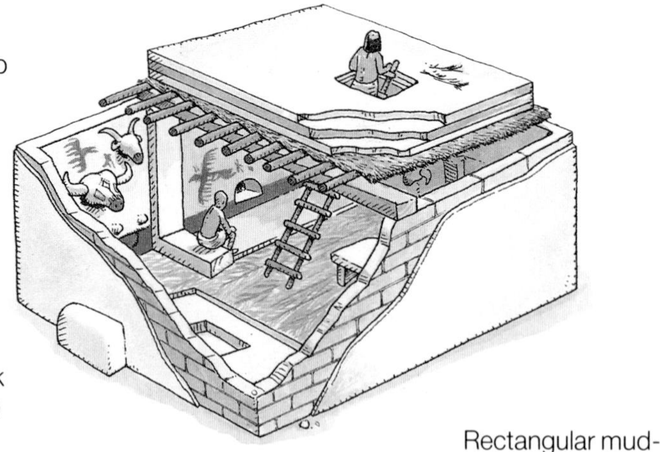

Each house butted up to the next for protection.

House at Catal Huyuk (Turkey) around 6500 BC. The people here were cattle-herders.

Rectangular mud-brick houses.

First writing

The first people to write instead of just drawing pictures were the Sumerians of Mesopotamia in about 3500 BC. They made wedge-shaped or cuneiform marks to stand for words such as 'cow' or 'sun'. By 1500 BC, the Chinese had invented a writing system with 50,000 word-signs.

First shorthand

A secretary to Cicero, the famous orator (speech-maker) of Ancient Rome, worked out how to do shorthand in about 50 BC. The secretary's name was Marcus Tullius Tiro.

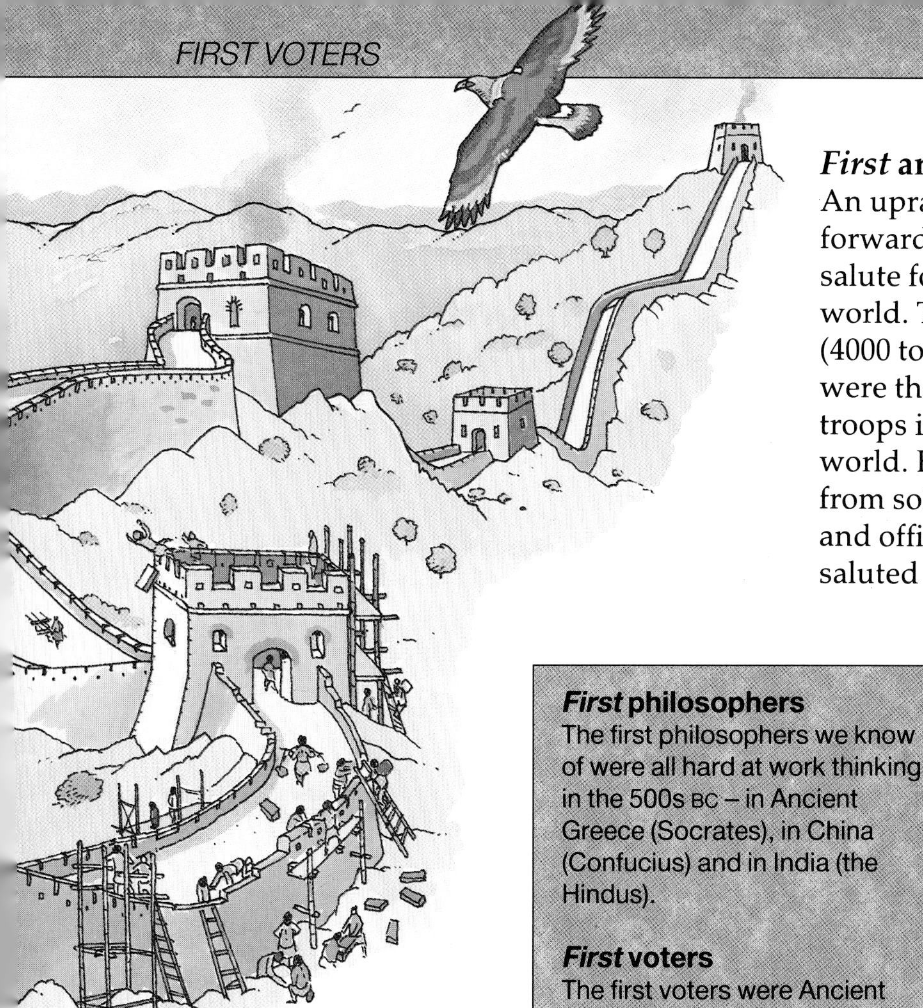

The Great Wall of China. There is a road along the top and guard-towers at intervals along the wall.

First army salute

An upraised hand, palm forwards, is a greeting or salute found all over the world. The Roman legions (4000 to 6000 soldiers) were the best-disciplined troops in the ancient world. Everyone saluted, from soldiers to centurions and officers. Generals saluted the emperor.

First philosophers

The first philosophers we know of were all hard at work thinking in the 500s BC – in Ancient Greece (Socrates), in China (Confucius) and in India (the Hindus).

First voters

The first voters were Ancient Greeks. They went to public meetings and voted by a show of hands. In some legal cases, votes were cast by using white or black balls, or by marked and unmarked shells.

First rule of Greek architecture

The Ancient Greeks believed that the most pleasing building shape was a rectangle, whose length and width conformed to the ratio 1 to 1.6 (for example, 100 metres × 160 metres long).

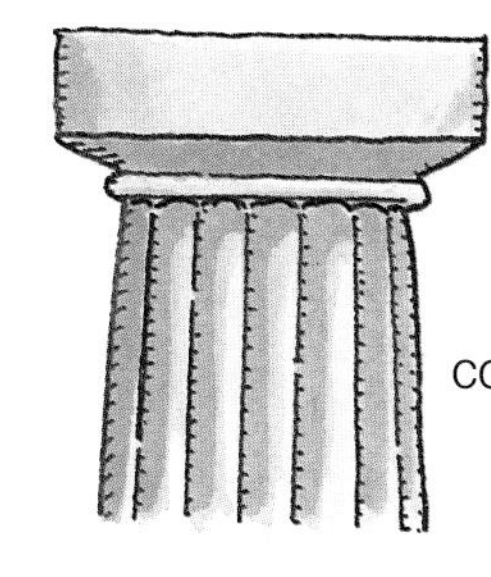

Doric capitals or columns, as seen in the Parthenon.

First European to try conquering India

European soldiers crossed the River Indus into India in 327 BC, led by the all-conquering Alexander the Great. Pursuing the defeated Persian emperor Darius across Asia Minor, Alexander saw the 'Gordian knot' that legend foretold only the conqueror of Asia would untie. Alexander slashed the knot free with his sword. Alexander never lost a battle, even when matched against Indian fighting elephants.

◁ Alexander The Great's army

Middle Ages – 1800

First Parliament
Iceland's parliament, the Althing, first met in AD 930. The Isle of Man's Tynewald claims to date from the 9th century. Britain's parliament began to grow in the 13th century.

First Norman to rule England

This was actually the first William I, or William the Conqueror, who conquered England in 1066. Normans developed a reputation for being good at government, cavalry charges and building castles.

First Mongol terror

The unstoppable Mongols led by Genghis Khan conquered north China by 1215. Then they charged west through Russia to Europe, slaughtering whole cities of people who resisted them. Genghis died in 1227 but the Mongols pressed on, laying waste to Hungary and Poland in 1241. Western Europe was there for the taking, but then Genghis's son died, and they retreated.

First African Empires

Africa's first and greatest empire was what we call Ancient Egypt, formed around 3100 BC, when Upper and Lower Egypt joined under King Menes. Its power was greatest around 1400 BC. Further south the kingdom of Kush flourished through trade from 2000 BC to AD 350. Other African empires included Ghana, Mali and Songhai, which flourished from AD 1000 to 1600.

People of ancient Nok (500 BC–AD 200) (now in Nigeria) made Africa's oldest known sculpture. The human heads all have pierced ears and hollow eyes.

First Crusade

Christian soldiers first left Europe in 1096 to help defend Constantinople from the Turks, and so started the First Crusade. From there they marched onward to Jerusalem, capturing it from Muslim rule in 1099.

Vasco da Gama

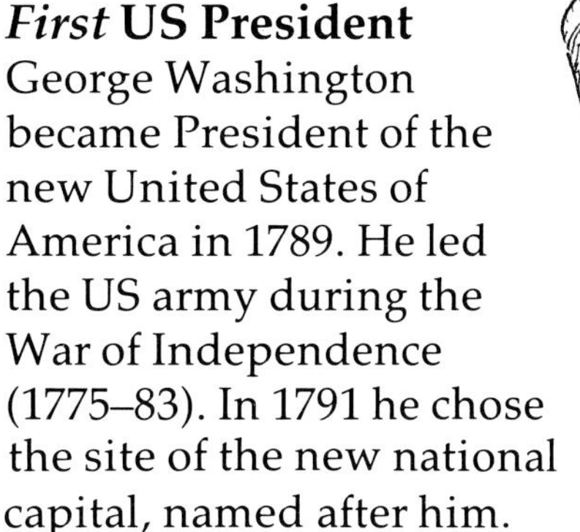

First US President

George Washington became President of the new United States of America in 1789. He led the US army during the War of Independence (1775–83). In 1791 he chose the site of the new national capital, named after him.

First Europeans across the Indian Ocean

The Portuguese sent four ships into the unknown in July 1497. In command was Vasco da Gama, with orders to sail south around Africa and head east. After the Cape Verde Islands, no land came into view for three months. But they reached the Cape of Good Hope, rested, and sailed into the Indian Ocean. Da Gama came home with only one third of his men in July 1499.

First colonies of America

The first permanent British settlement in North America was at Jamestown, founded in 1607, which grew into the colony of Virginia. With Maryland (settled by Catholics) it was one of the earliest colonies. Puritans founded those in New England. St Augustine in Florida, is the USA's oldest city, found by the Spanish in 1565.

First king-killer mole

The mole whose molehill tripped up William III's horse was toasted by the Jacobites (supporters of the king's rivals, the Stuarts). William was thrown, and died on 8 March 1702.

First Tudor queen on the block

Tudor England was dangerous for queens, especially for wives of King Henry VIII. Anne Boleyn (his second wife) was the first to be beheaded, in 1536.

First Mogul Emperor

A prince of Afghanistan named Babar (the Tiger) conquered northern India in 1526 and became the first Mogul (or Muslim) emperor. He had two famous conquering ancestors: Tamerlane and Genghis Khan.

First guillotine execution

French doctor Joseph Guillotin designed the guillotine as a quick and efficient way of killing people. On April 25 1792, a highwayman called Nicolas Pelletier became the guillotine's first victim. It was kept busy in the French Revolution's Reign of Terror (1793–94), when 180,000 death sentences were passed.

Modern World

First wagons roll West
Settlers in creaking 'prairie schooners' set out for the West (beyond the Mississippi River) as the USA began to expand westwards in the 1840s. The Oregon Trail winding 3000 kilometres across the Great Plains and the Rocky Mountains was long and difficult. But dust, bad weather and disease were usually worse problems than attacks by hostile Indians.

First trans-America railroad
Rail tracks across America were joined at Promontory Point in Utah on 10 May 1869. The Union Pacific Railroad began laying track west from Omaha, Nebraska, in 1863. In 1865, the Central Pacific Railroad began building east from Sacramento, California.

First trade unions
Workers formed the first unions in the late 1700s. Until 1824, unions were banned in Britain, and they were not recognized in the USA until the 1840s.

First shots of American Civil War
Confederate guns opened fire on Fort Sumter in Charleston, South Carolina on 12 April 1861. Inside, were 68 Union soldiers loyal to President Lincoln. Watching Southerners cheered the first shell. After 34 hours the fort surrendered. No one died in this first battle of a long and bitter war.

First World War
The war that started in Europe in August 1914 was the first war to involve the whole world. Most of the fighting was in Europe, but conflict spread to the Middle East, Asia and Africa.

First Russian revolution
The first Russian revolution was in 1905. It failed to overthrow the Tsar. In 1917, Russia collapsed into chaos. There was a second revolution led by Lenin, and this time the Tsar fell from power.

Lenin, first leader of the Soviet Union

First Fascist dictators

The Fascist Benito Mussolini became leader of Italy's government in 1922. Germany went Fascist in 1933, under Hitler.

First votes for women

New Zealand was the first country to give women the same voting rights as men in 1893. Women had voted in 1869 in the Territory of Wyoming, USA, and in the Isle of Man in 1881. Swiss women did not gain the vote until 1971.

The cause of ▷ women's suffrage gained momentum through the 1800s. Suffragettes were prepared to break the law to attract attention to their campaign.

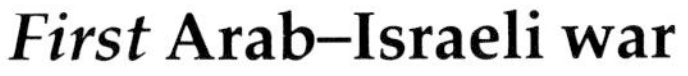

First Arab–Israeli war

The first Arab–Israeli war broke out the day after Israel came into being in 1948. Many Jews from Europe saw Palestine as their ancient homeland. But for centuries Palestine had been Arab land.

Martin Luther King

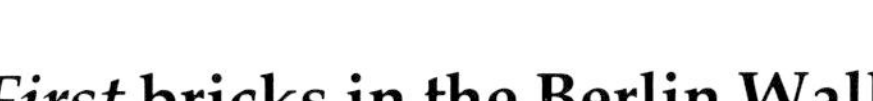

First bricks in the Berlin Wall

On 13 August 1961, East German police began building the Berlin Wall. This concrete and wire symbol of the Cold War stood until 1989.

First president of Russia

The Soviet Union ended on Christmas Day 1991. Fifteen states became independent republics. The biggest of these new countries, Russia, was led by President Boris Yeltsin.

First great civil rights march

Slavery ended in the USA in 1865, but Black Americans still struggled for equal rights. The Civil Rights movement gained pace in the 1950s. In 1963, Martin Luther King led 200,000 protesters on a march in Washington DC.

EXPLORERS

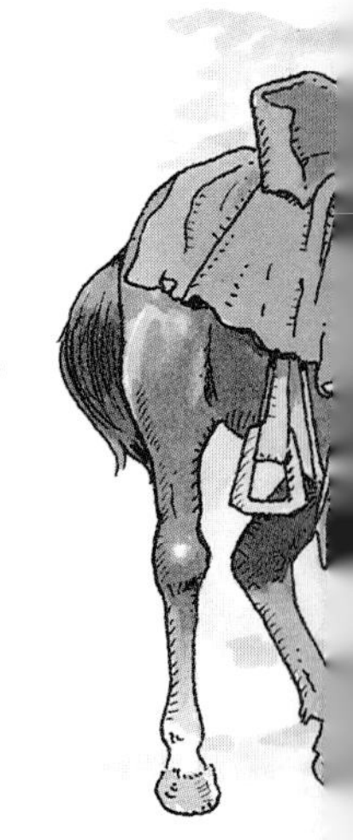

Mountains and deserts were natural barriers to explorers. The oceans seem an even more formidable challenge. But it was by sea that most of the first great explorers travelled into the unknown.

New World

First Greek to visit Britain

In 300 BC, a Greek sea captain called Pytheas sailed his galley along the shores of Britain. He had come from Marseilles, braving the cold northern ocean as far as a country he called 'Ultima Thule' which was probably Norway.

First European settlers in North America

Leif Ericsson took his Viking longship west from Greenland in 1002. Finally he reached 'Vinland' (Newfoundland). The hardy Vikings founded colonies in North America, but these later died out.

First to see Columbus's New World

Rodrigo Triano was the first sailor in Columbus's 1492 expedition to sight land, 36 days after leaving Spain. The crew's first landing point in the New World was Watling Island in the Bahamas.

◁ Columbus's flagship *Santa Maria* was 24 metres long and had 40 people on board. His other two ships, *Niña* and *Pinta*, were smaller.

◁ Carved dragon prow of a Viking ship. It had oars and a single sail.

First European look at the Pacific Ocean

In 1513, Vasco Nunez de Balboa crossed the jungles and swamps of Panama from the Atlantic coast. He gazed upon a wide, seemingly peaceful sea. It was the biggest ocean on Earth, and was unknown to Europe.

First sailor into the St Lawrence River

Frenchman Jacques Cartier sailed up the St Lawrence River in Canada in 1536, hoping it would lead him to China and the Indies! Europeans of the 1500s were convinced that Asia was close to America.

Jacques Cartier (1491–1557) claimed New France (Canada) for his country.

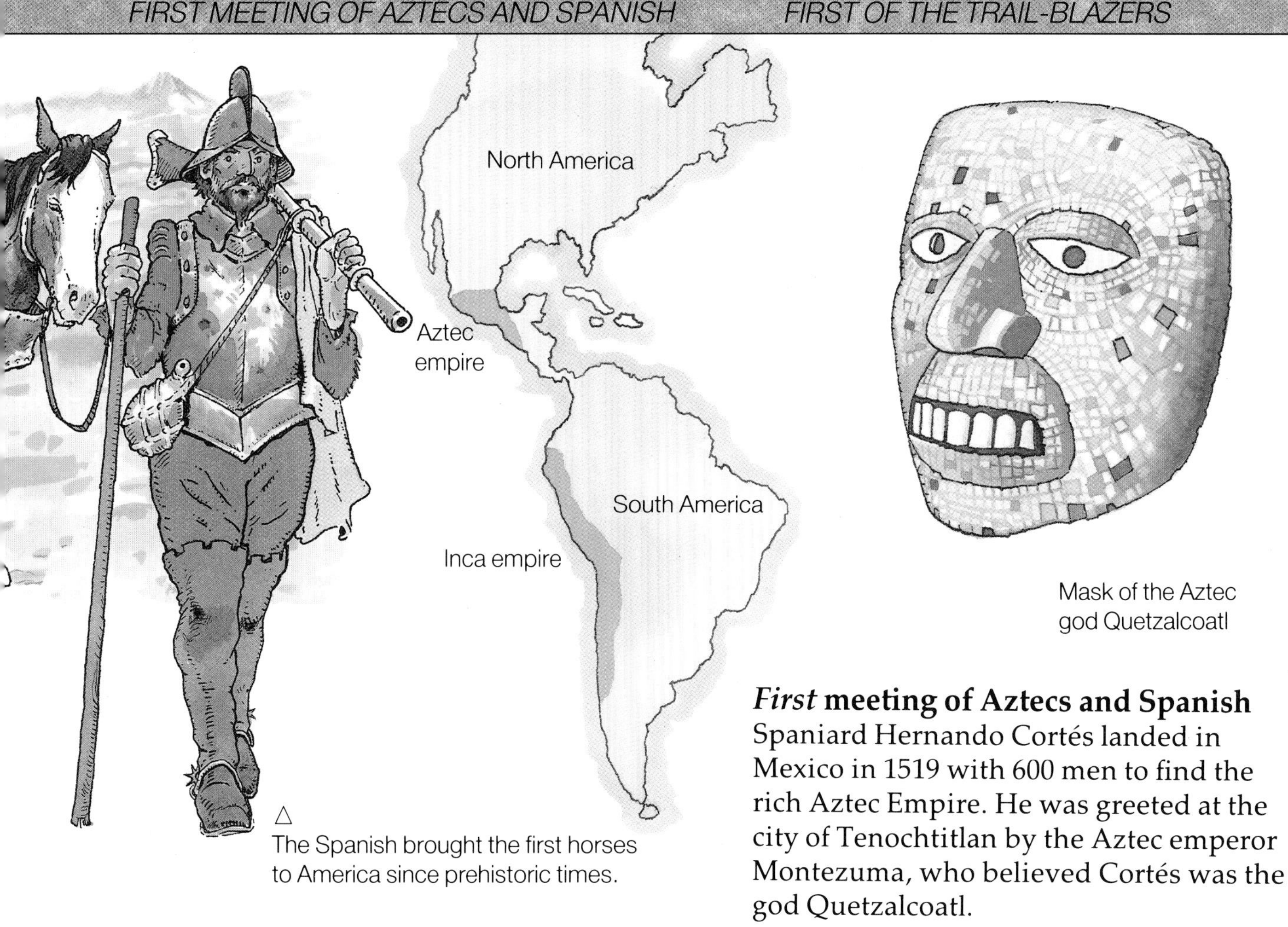

△
The Spanish brought the first horses to America since prehistoric times.

Mask of the Aztec god Quetzalcoatl

***First* meeting of Aztecs and Spanish**
Spaniard Hernando Cortés landed in Mexico in 1519 with 600 men to find the rich Aztec Empire. He was greeted at the city of Tenochtitlan by the Aztec emperor Montezuma, who believed Cortés was the god Quetzalcoatl.

***First* white men to the Mississippi**
Hernando de Soto led a small army of Spaniards inland from Florida in search of gold in 1539. Instead they found the mighty Mississippi River.

***First* of the trail-blazers**
Before the wagons rolled west to California in the 1840s, fur traders like Jedediah Smith blazed trails from Great Salt Lake across the Mojave Desert and Rocky Mountains to California. Smith crossed the Rockies three times before 1831.

***First* to map the West**
Meriwether Lewis and William Clark travelled 13,000 kilometres up the Mississippi, across the Rockies, along the Columbia River to the Pacific in 1804–06. They were the first scientific explorers of the American West.

Lewis and Clark surveyed and mapped the West.

Africa, Asia and Pacific

First Chinese grand tour

The Chinese admiral Cheng Ho commanded the largest expeditions ever seen, between 1405 and 1433. The biggest of these, in 1431, numbered 27,000 men in 300 sailing junks. The Chinese visited the East Indies, India and East Africa.

First great Arab traveller

Ibn Battuta made his first journey as a 21-year-old Muslim pilgrim from Morocco to Mecca in 1325. He made a rule 'never to travel any road a second time'. Later wanderings through the Muslim world took him to Africa, Spain, India, Russia and China. He became a celebrity, journeying by boat and overland a distance of 120,000 kilometres, and wrote a famous book about his travels.

First around the world

In 1519, five ships and 277 men sailed west from Spain, under the command of Ferdinand Magellan. One ship and 19 men arrived home from the east in 1522. They had made the first voyage around the world.

Cheng Ho saw many strange animals.

ginger

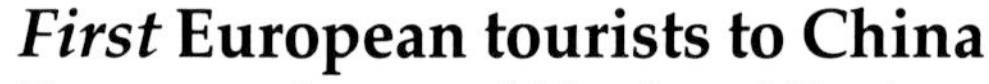

First European tourists to China

Two merchants of Venice, Nicolo and Maffeo Polo, went to China in 1271. This was their second trip to Asia, and with them went Nicolo's son Marco. It was 24 years before they returned.

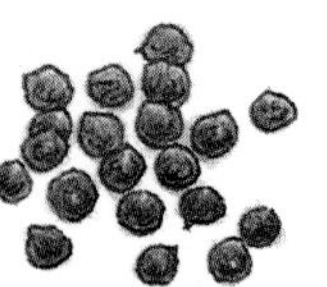

pepper

cloves

nutmeg

mace

Europeans brought spices from Asia.

First Pacific voyagers

Many Pacific islands were settled thousands of years ago by seafarers from Asia. The Maoris sailed in canoes to New Zealand before AD 800.

△ A canoe from south-east Papua

First European to see a kangaroo

A Dutch captain called Dirk Hartog may have seen a kangaroo in 1616 when he landed in western Australia. Cook's expedition artist sketched kangaroos in 1770.

First trans-Australia explorers

In 1860, Robert O'Hara Burke set out from Melbourne to cross Australia. He succeeded in 1861, but on the return journey Burke and two men died. The sole survivor was cared for by Aborigines and later rescued.

Cook first meets the Maoris

Captain James Cook sailed to New Zealand in 1769. His British crew first met the Maoris at Poverty Bay, where the tattooed locals were unfriendly. Cook sailed around both of New Zealand's islands in his ship *Endeavour*, and found other Maoris friendlier.

First lady of African exploration

Tucking up her long skirts when necessary, Mary Kingsley (1862–1900) was one of the few women to explore Africa alone when it was still the 'Unknown Continent' to Europeans. She travelled to West Africa, studying natural history and writing books about Africa and its people.

Firsts in African exploration

2500 BC	Egyptians explore Somalia.
400s BC	Hanno of Carthage sails as far south as Senegal.
1300	Ibn Battuta travels through Muslim central and west Afria.
1487	Bartomoleu Diaz of Portugal is first to sail to the southern tip of Africa and see the Indian Ocean.
1828	Rene Caille of France is first European to cross the Sahara.
1849–73	David Livingstone explores central Africa
1858	John Hanning Speke discovers Lake Victoria
1889	Henry Morton Stanley follows the Congo River (now called the Zaire) to the Atlantic.

Stanley was sent to find the ▷ 'lost' Livingstone. He found him at Ujiji (Tanzania) in 1871 and the meeting made world headlines.

◁ Alexander Laing was the first European to visit Timbuktu (Mali) in 1826. Two years later Rene Caille saw, and drew, the fabled city.

Poles, Space, Mountains, Undersea

First to the North Pole?

On 21 April 1909, US Commander Robert E. Peary reached the North Pole with Matthew Henson. Dr Frederick Cook claimed that he had got there the year before. Peary was believed. Maybe neither Peary nor Cook got there. Both claimed to have crossed the ice faster than modern polar travellers have been able to do.

First sub-polar sub

The world's first nuclear submarine, USS *Nautilus*, passed under the North Pole ice in 1958. Three US submarines surfaced at the Pole in 1986.

First climbers of Everest

First to the top of the world's highest mountain, in 1953, were New Zealand's Edmund Hillary and Nepal's Sherpa Tenzing Norgay.

Tenzing on Everest, ▷ 8863 metres above sea level.

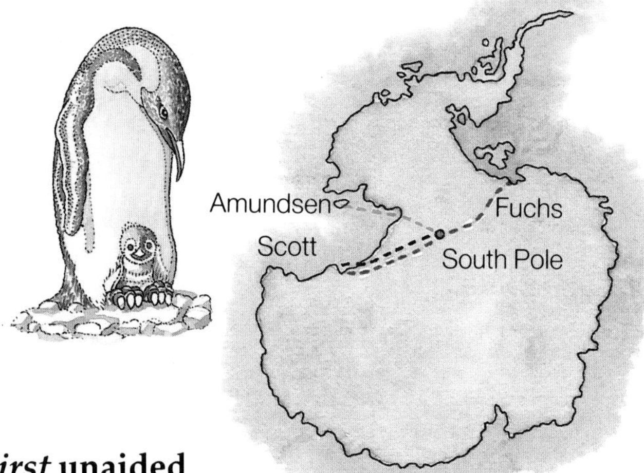

First to the South Pole

Norwegian Roald Amundsen and four companions reached the South Pole on 14 December 1911. A month behind came five British, led by Captain Robert Falcon Scott, who died on the return trip. The first lone walker to the South Pole was another Norwegian, Erling Kagge, who finished a 50-day sledge trek in January 1993.

First unaided walk across Antarctica

Sir Ranulph Fiennes and Dr Michael Stroud completed the longest unsupported ski-walk across Antarctica in 1993. They reached the South Pole in just over two months, and continued to cross the frozen continent.

First Antarctic crossing

A 1958 Commonwealth expedition led by Vivian Fuchs of Britain made the first land crossing of Antarctica in 99 days. Over 3400 kilometres tested the tracked vehicles to their limit.

First deep-space probe
The unmanned US spacecraft, Pioneer 10, launched in 1972, left the solar system in 1983.

First moon walker
The first feet to tread Moon dust belonged to *Apollo 11* astronaut Neil Armstrong. On 20 July 1969, lunar module *Eagle* landed on the Moon. Out stepped Armstrong, who said 'That's one small step for man, one giant leap for mankind'.

First aqualung
The aqualung or scuba-diving breathing gear was developed in the 1940s by the French undersea explorer Jacques-Yves Cousteau with Emile Gagnan.

First planet named Len Carter
Astronomers spotted this 10-kilometre wide lump of rock in 1979. In 1988 the mini-planet was named Len Carter, after the secretary of the British Inter-Planetary Society.

First to the ocean bottom
In 1960, Jacques Piccard and Dan Walsh sank 10,916 metres in the bathyscaphe Trieste into the Marianas Trench in the Pacific – the deepest point in the World's oceans.

First spaceman
Yuri Gagarin was a spaceman for 108 minutes, while his Soviet *Vostok 1* spacecraft made one orbit of the Earth on 12 April 1961.

First crash on the Moon
Soviet spacecraft *Luna 2* crashed into the Moon in 1959. Later that year, *Luna 3* photographed the far, dark side of the moon for the first time.

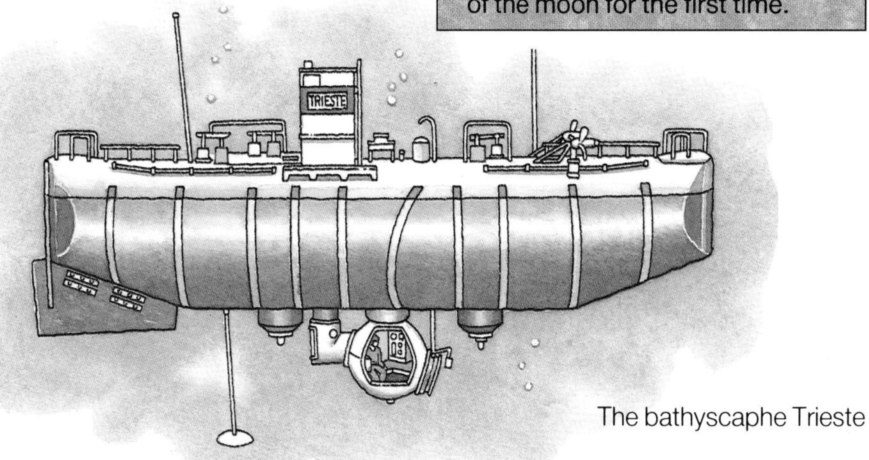

The bathyscaphe Trieste

ARTS AND ENTERTAINMENT

Art and entertainment began when people first sang, danced and painted the walls of their cave-homes. The first artists may have been magicians as well. And the best of art certainly has magic.

Literature, Drama, Cinema

First stories

Literature began when people first told stories. Later they wrote down epic poems such as the Greek *Iliad* and the Assyrian tale of Gilgamesh (700s–600s BC).

First play-watchers

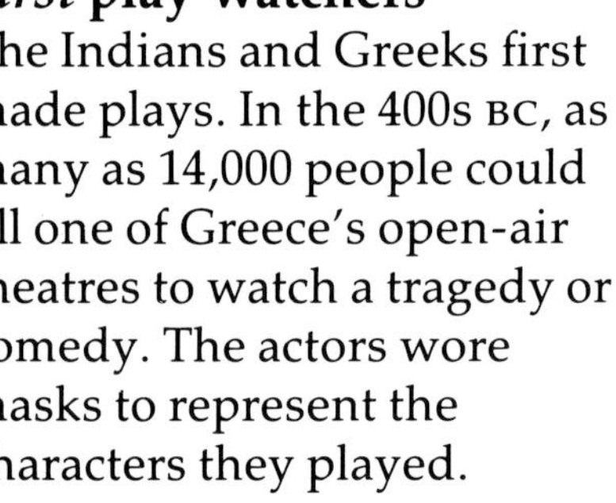

The Indians and Greeks first made plays. In the 400s BC, as many as 14,000 people could fill one of Greece's open-air theatres to watch a tragedy or comedy. The actors wore masks to represent the characters they played.

First monster story

Many ancient stories have monsters – the Old English poem *Beowulf* (AD 700–750) has a nasty one. The first modern horror-hero was Frankenstein's monster, created in Mary Shelley's book of 1818.

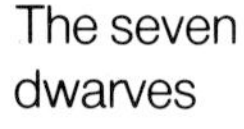

The seven dwarves ▽

First Grimm fairy tales

Two brothers called Grimm, who were both German scholars, collected old stories. They published some in 1815, including 'Cinderella', 'The Sleeping Beauty' and 'Snow White'.

First novel

Most literature was written in verse until the 1500s. The novel first made prose popular for story-telling. One of the first great novels was *Don Quixote*, written in 1605 by the Spaniard Miguel de Cervantes.

First Romeo in Tibet

A miner wooed Juliet in the first Tibetan production of Shakespeare's *Romeo and Juliet* in 1981.

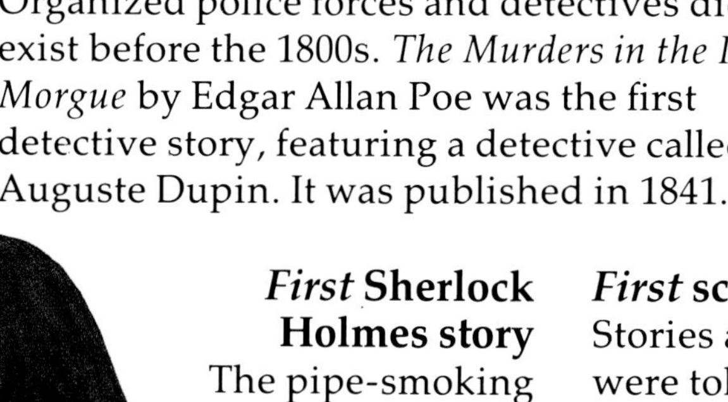

◁ Verne's Moon-voyagers, in a giant cannon shell

First detective story

Organized police forces and detectives did not exist before the 1800s. *The Murders in the Rue Morgue* by Edgar Allan Poe was the first detective story, featuring a detective called Auguste Dupin. It was published in 1841.

First Sherlock Holmes story

The pipe-smoking detective first appeared in 'A Study in Scarlet' written by Arthur Conan Doyle for the *Strand* Magazine in 1891.

First science fiction

Stories about trips to the Moon were told thousands of years ago, but science fiction really began with Jules Verne (1825–1905). His books include *Twenty Thousand Leagues Under the Sea* and *From the Earth to the Moon*.

Firsts in Cinema

First feature film with synchronized sound: *The Jazz Singer* (1927)

First film to win 11 Oscars (all-time record): *Ben Hur* (1959)

First star to win four Oscars: Katharine Hepburn (1934, 1969, 1969, 1982)

First five-year-old to win an Oscar: Shirley Temple (1934)

First film to cost over 100 million dollars: *Terminator 2 – Judgement Day* (1991)

First movie camera

Edison's kinetograph of 1890 was the first practical movie camera. Later cameras used by the movie industry were too big for home use. Smaller cameras made home movies popular from the 1920s, and from the 1980s anyone could make videos with lightweight camcorders.

First paperbacks

Soft-cover books (such as pamphlets) were common in the 1600s. The modern paperback, originally cheap and pocket-sized, dates from the 1930s, with Albatrosses (Germany 1932), Penguins (UK 1935) and Pocket Books (USA 1939).

First starring role for Mickey Mouse

Walt Disney's famous mouse was first called Mortimer. Renamed Mickey, he squeaked into movie history in the 1928 cartoon *Steamboat Willie*. Donald Duck first quacked in 1934, and Mickey and Donald both appeared later that year in *The Band Concert*.

First cinema show

Customers in New York's 'Kinetoscope and Parlor' watched films flicker on Edison's new machines in 1894. In 1895 in Paris, the Lumière brothers opened the first movie theatre with a screen, the Cinématographe.

Music, Painting, Sculpture

First music
The first musicians sang or chanted, and to keep time they banged hollow sticks as drums. Drums were also good for dancing and for making warriors feel brave before a hunt or a battle. The oldest drums found are made of clay and are 6000 years old, but drumming began long before, as did pipe-blowing, at least 12,000 years ago. By 4000 years ago, musicians were playing stringed instruments such as the harp and lyre.

First saxophone
The Belgian Adolphe Saxe gave his name to the saxophone. He made the first one in the 1840s. The saxophone is a brass instrument blown through a reed, like a woodwind instrument.

First piano
Bartolommeo Cristofori (1665–1731) built the first piano in 1709. Its wire strings were hit by hammers. In the earlier harpsichord, the strings were plucked. John Broadwood invented the piano pedals in 1783.

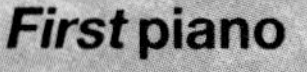

First music tour by boy genius
The composer Wolfgang Amadeus Mozart (1756–1791) was writing music at the age of five. He played the violin and piano superbly. His father took him on a musical tour round the courts of Europe. Mozart published his first compositions at the age of eight and had written the first of his 41 symphonies before he was 13.

First opera
Opera began in Italy, which has been the home of opera ever since. The first opera we know much about was *Dafne*, performed during the Florence Carnival of 1597. The music was composed by the Italian, Jacopo Peri.

First paints
Stone Age cave-artists made their colours from vegetable and earth pigments mixed with water or animal fat. The Ancient Egyptians added resins and drying oils to their paints. Oil paints became popular in Europe in the 1500s.

First artists

The earliest paintings still visible are in caves in southern France and northern Spain. Cave artists painted animals, perhaps as a form of magic to bring good hunting.

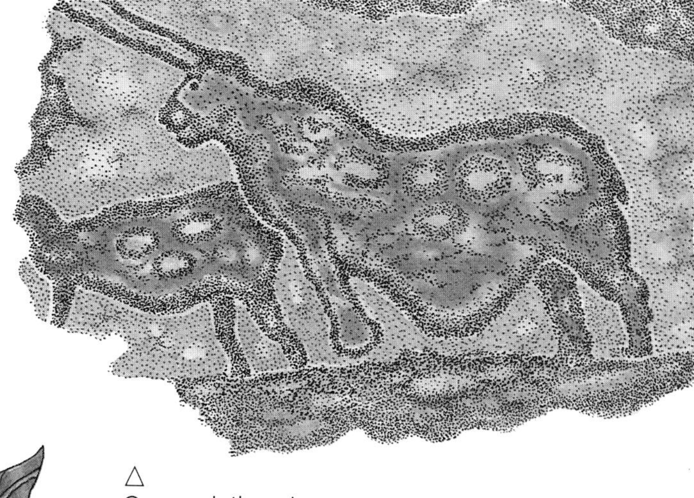

△ Cave painting at Lascaux in France from 18,000 BC

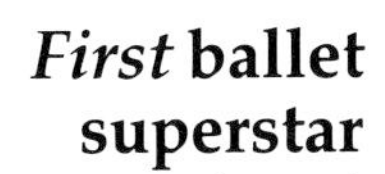

First ballet superstar

Russia has produced many great dancers but none more exciting than Vaslav Nijinsky (1890–1950). He seemed to 'hang' in mid air while making dazzling leaps about the stage.

◁ Nijinsky in the ballet L'Apres Midi d'un Faune, 1912.

The Venus of Willendorf

First sculpture

People of 30,000 years ago made figures by carving wood, stone or bone. This figure was probably a life-giving Mother Goddess.

First artists with perspective

Perspective makes paintings look as if they are three-dimensional. The Greeks and Romans knew how to draw in perspective, but the art was forgotten in Europe until around 1400, when painters of the Renaissance studied art scientifically.

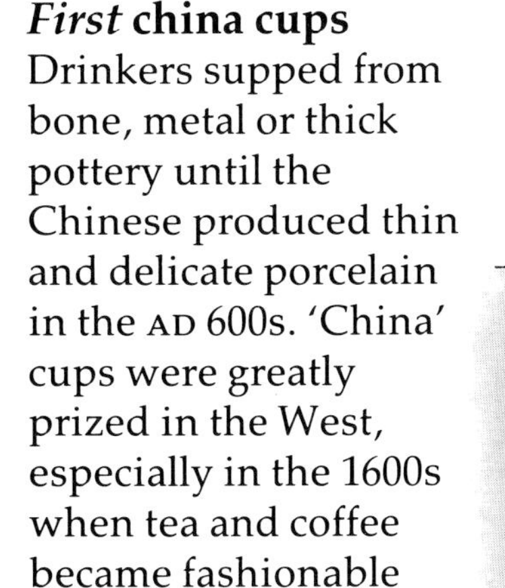

First china cups

Drinkers supped from bone, metal or thick pottery until the Chinese produced thin and delicate porcelain in the AD 600s. 'China' cups were greatly prized in the West, especially in the 1600s when tea and coffee became fashionable drinks.

In perspective drawing, distant objects are shown smaller and closer together.

First pencils

Graphite pencils with wooden casings came into use in the late 1700s.

Popular Entertainment

First Colosseum spectacular

In AD 80, over 50,000 people crowded daily into the new Colosseum in Rome. They came to watch gladiators and wild animals fight and die, and to marvel at mock sea battles staged in the flooded arena. This was mass entertainment Roman-style.

To die or not to die? The Emperor's signal meant life or death for a gladiator defeated in the arena.

First circuses

Philip Astley drew the crowds to his Amphitheatre of Arts in London in 1769. The show featured horse-riding, fireworks and historical pageants. Rival showmen chose the shorter name 'circus'.

First female pop megastar

No other female singer has matched the record sales of Madonna. In 1986 she was the first woman to top both single and album charts. Her *True Blue* album was No. 1 in 28 countries.

First radio broadcasts

Music was heard over the radio as early as 1906 in the USA. In Britain, station 2MT in Essex began regular entertainment broadcasts in 1922, and the BBC first broadcast the 6 o'clock news in the same year.

First stars

First juggler to juggle seven clubs, Albert Petrovski of Russia (1963)

First video recordings—on 78 rpm discs (1928). Videotape first tried (1956).

First appearance of Winnie-the-Pooh: (1926). This was some way behind Peter Rabbit (1902).

First singles record charts: (USA, 1940), (UK, 1952).

First roller-coaster (1816)

First digital compact cassette

DCCS (digital compact cassettes) went on sale in 1992. They offer sound quality to match that of compact discs, first sold in 1982.

First crossword puzzle

On 21 December 1913, *New York World* newspaper published a new puzzle. Its Across and Down word-clues are now beloved by crossword addicts the world over.

First yo-yo

The yo-yo was an aristocrat's toy of the 1700s, but became a twentieth-century craze in 1929.

First synthesizer

The first experimental synthesizer was invented in 1953. The Moog synthesizer (1964) became a favourite with many pop musicians.

First Christmas card

Hand-painted for Sir Henry Cole of London in 1843 by an artist friend, the first card was too expensive for most people. Cheap printed cards became popular from the 1870s.

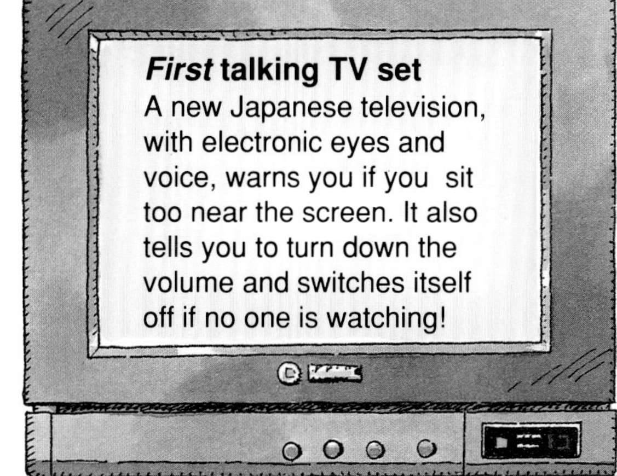

First talking TV set

A new Japanese television, with electronic eyes and voice, warns you if you sit too near the screen. It also tells you to turn down the volume and switches itself off if no one is watching!

A modern roller-coaster

First Michael Jackson hit: *I Want You Back* (1970), as an 11-year-old member of the Jackson Five. His *Thriller* album is the all-time best-seller.

First to walk Niagara Falls on a high wire: Blondin (1859).

First television commercial—for a watch, (USA, 1941)

Most successful movie (box office money). *ET: The Extra-Terrestial* (1982)

SPORTS AND PASTIMES

The earliest sports of hunting, racing and martial arts trained good warriors. These developed into the ball games of Ancient Egypt, Greek athletics, Persian hockey and football of the Middle Ages.

First board games

The Persians played board games in 3000 BC. Chess was played in India 2000 years ago.

First card games

Packs of cards had reached Europe from the East by 1300. Early packs had 78 cards. The 'modern' four-suit, 52-card pack dates from the 1500s.

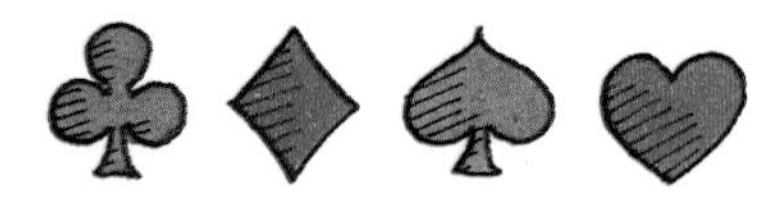

First football

Football was popular in the Middle Ages, so much so that it was banned in England as it stopped men from practising archery.

First rugby player

In 1823, William Webb Ellis was so bored while playing football at Rugby School that he picked up the ball and ran with it.

First polo

Polo was played in Persia around 500 BC. Riders sometimes used the heads of slain enemies as balls.

First baseball

The New York Nines beat the Knickerbockers in 1846, in the first recognized baseball game.

First basketball

Modern basketball dates from 1891. It was thought up by James Naismith.

First cricket international

The first Test match took place in 1877 when Australia beat England.

First Olympics

The Olympic Games were first held in Greece from 776 BC to AD 393. The modern games began in 1896, and are held every four years. The coloured rings symbolize the five continents of the Earth.

First Marathon

In 490 BC Pheidippides, a Greek, ran 40 kilometres to report victory over Persia at Marathon.

First World Cup

The first soccer World Cup was won by Uruguay in 1930. Brazil, Italy and West Germany have all won the championship three times.

First female tennis star

Suzanne Lenglen (1899–1938) was beaten only once in matches between 1919 and 1926. She won the Wimbledon singles' title six times.

***First* horse races**
Greek horsemen raced in the Ancient Olympics, and the Romans staged races before big crowds. The first race meetings in Britain were held in the 1540s.

***First* Winter Olympics**
Skiiers and ski-jumpers from 18 nations went to Chamonix in France for the first Winter Olympics in 1924.

***First* women's cricket match**
In 1745 in Surrey, England, a team of 'eleven maids' from Bramley played a team from Hambleton.

***First* club golfers**
The Gentlemen Golfers of Edinburgh, Scotland, started in 1744 and is probably the oldest club. The game of golf itself goes back at least to 1457.

***First* two-way Channel swim**
The first both-ways swim, by Antonio Abertondo of Argentina in 1961, took over 43 hours. Philip Rush of New Zealand did it in 16 hours in 1987, and completed a three-way crossing in 28 hours 21 minutes.

***First* black athletics superstar**
Sprinter and long-jumper Jesse Owens of the USA won four events at the 1936 Berlin Olympics.

Sporting firsts
First American football: (1869)
First solo row across the Atlantic: John Fairfax (1969)
First rodeo star to wrestle steers: Bill Picket (1900)
First fencers: crossed swords in Egypt about 1200 BC.
First darts: thrown as weapons in ancient battles.
First roller skates: worn to a London ball in 1760 by Joseph Merlin, who crashed when unable to stop.
First Japanese sumo wrestlers: sweated and strained in about 23 BC.

***First* superbowl**
American football's greatest occasion dates from 1967.

***First* Davis Cup holders**
The USA won the first tennis Davis Cup in 1900.

***First* five-Games medal winner**
Raisa Smetanina from Russia won her tenth Olympic medal in skiing in 1992. She was the first athlete to win medals at five Games (1976–92).

***First* seven-gold-medal Olympian**
American swimmer, Mark Spitz, won seven gold medals at the 1972 Olympics.

***First* Grand Prix motor race**
The French Grand Prix dates from 1906 and is the world's oldest.

A 1906 Renault

***First* 100 metres in 10 seconds**
Jim Hines (USA) recorded a time of 9.95 seconds at the 1968 Olympic Games.

***First* Derby**
This English horse race was first run in 1780.

PEOPLE AND PLACES

From the ancient pyramids to the supermarket trolley of today, civilization has come far. Places change people and people alter places. The marvellous and the ridiculous exist together, side by side.

First Royal residence

The British monarch's chief residence outside London is Windsor Castle, the biggest castle still used as a home. From an earthwork begun by William the Conqueror, it now boasts 15 towers of thick stone. The oldest parts were built in the 1300s. The big round keep or central tower dates from 1528. The castle was badly damaged by a fire in 1992.

First Wonders of the World

First of the Seven Wonders of the Ancient World were the pyramids of Khufu, Khafre and Menkaure at Giza in Egypt, built between 2600–2500 BC. They have lasted while other Wonders crumbled.

First scuba marathons

The first underwater Channel swim was in 1962. In 1987, six divers swam 152 kilometres up and down a pool.

First universities

The first university students attended colleges in Fez, Morocco in AD 859 and Bologna, Italy in 1088. There were much earlier schools for senior students, in Greece and India.

First supermarket

In 1930, Michael Cullin opened the first supermarket, in America. Customers served themselves from a wide range of goods in one store. Trolley-pushing became an everyday part of shopping.

△ Queen Victoria's saloon carriage of 1869. It contained a special handle which could modify the speed of the train.

First royal train trip

Queen Victoria made her first journey by steam train in 1842, from Windsor to Paddington Station in London.

First bathing costumes

Sea bathing became popular in the late 1700s as a health-cure. Bathers dipped naked. By the 1850s however, this was thought indecent, and so bathers covered themselves in all-over bathing costumes.

Firsts among leaders

First Roman emperor: Augustus (27 BC–AD 14)

First tsar of all Russia: Ivan IV, the Terrible (1530–84)

First king of Great Britain: James I (1603–1625)

First king of England to lose his head: Charles I (1649)

First British prime minister: Sir Robert Walpole (1721)

First US president to be assassinated: Lincoln (1865)

First prime minister of India: Jawarharlal Nehru (1947–64).

First woman prime minister: Mrs Bandaranaike of Ceylon, now Sri Lanka (1960)

First US President to resign: Richard Nixon (1969–74)

First US President who was formerly a film star, also the oldest when elected (69): Ronald Reagan (1981–89).

First doll-designing missile man

The man who made the Barbie doll in 1957, US inventor-extraordinary Jack Ryan, had other ideas that went with a bang. He was also creator of the Hawk and Sparrow missiles.

First slot machine

Amusement arcades are a modern idea, but the Ancient Greeks had a machine that worked on the same principle. Visitors to sacred shrines put a token into the machine, which then dispensed holy water.

First package holidays

Only wealthy people holidayed abroad until the 1800s. Thomas Cook started a business to escort British groups abroad, sending his first tour to Paris in 1861.

First solo climb of Everest

Reinhold Messner (Italy) made the first lone ascent of Mt. Everest in 1980.

First shop signs

In a Roman street, a bunch of vines advertised a wine shop and a boot was hung outside a shoe-shop.

People and Places 2

First railway fatality
As crowds cheered the opening of Britain's Liverpool and Manchester Railway in 1830, William Huskisson MP was knocked down and killed by a train.

First spiritualist medium
The Fox sisters of New York became famous in 1848 for receiving messages from the dead. Mrs Hayden became the first professional medium in 1852.

First money
Coins replaced shells, beads and other tokens in Lydia (now Turkey) about 630 BC. The Chinese had paper money by the AD 800s.

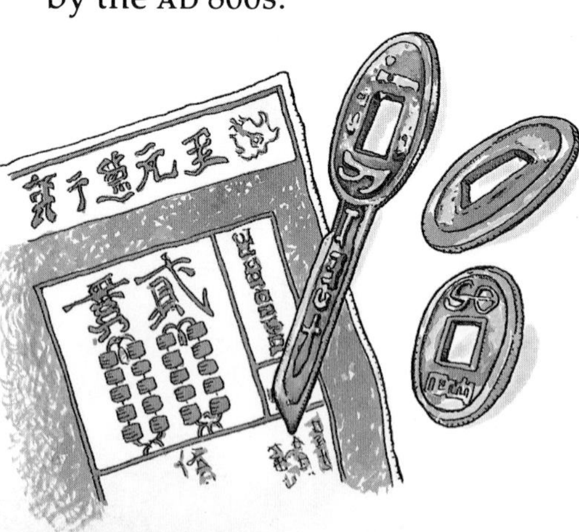

First woman driver
Berta Benz, wife of Karl, helped him to build the first car in 1885. She drove the car on its first cross-country trip in 1888, buying petrol at a chemist's shop.

First hammocks
Columbus's crew saw American Indians using bark hammocks and adopted the idea for sleeping aboard ship.

First Victoria Cross
Britain's highest award for gallantry in battle was first won by a Royal Navy lieutenant, Charles Lucas, in 1856. During the Crimean War, he threw a live Russian shell overboard.

Firsts Around the World

Smallest independent country: Vatican City State

Largest by land area: Russia

Largest by population: China

Biggest cities: Mexico City and Tokyo

Most ancient capital: Damascus (Syria).

Coldest place: Antarctica, minus 89 degrees centigrade.

Hottest: North Africa, where a temperature of 58 degrees centigrade was measured (Libya, 1922).

Thickest ice: about 4800 m in Antarctica.

Most car-crazy: USA (one vehicle for every 1½ people).

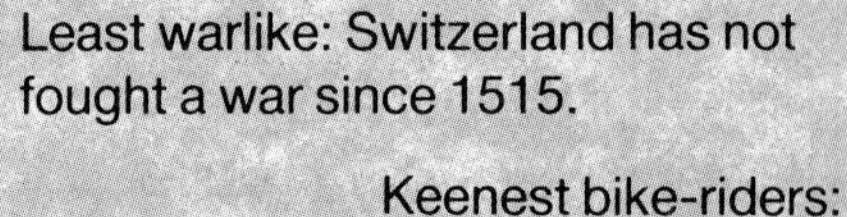

Least warlike: Switzerland has not fought a war since 1515.

Keenest bike-riders: The Chinese (more than 200 million cycles).

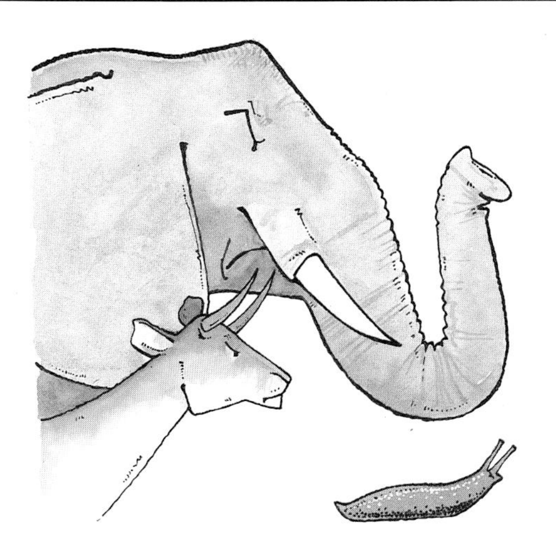

First menu offering roast eland and slug soup

Naturalist-surgeon Frank Buckland planned unusual meals in the mid-1800s. The menus included boiled elephant trunk, roast eland and slug soap. Buckland believed people should farm exotic animals to increase the nation's food resources.

Firsts in Fashion

First shoes: fur snowshoes (prehistoric), leather sandals (5000 BC).

First umbrella: the first rain-proof European umbrella was opened in 1637. The Chinese used them as sunshades much earlier.

First kilt: worn by Ancient Egyptian men.

First trousers: fitted clothes were first worn in Persia, where men wore trousers.

First full wigs: curled periwigs were fashionable from the 1660s.

First modern trousers: by 1820, Western men were switching from knee breeches to trousers.

First hair rollers: clay rollers were used in Ancient Greece.

First short skirts: Western women's knees emerged from beneath skirt hemlines in the 1920s.

First bras: in the 1930s, bras developed as a separate garment from the boned corsets of the 1800s.

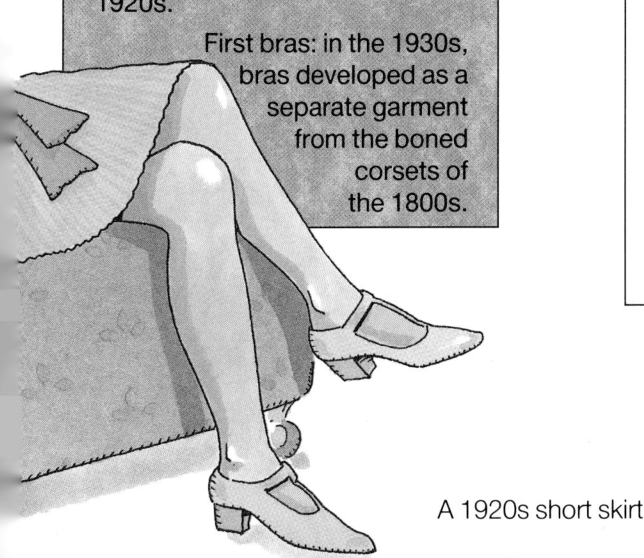

A 1920s short skirt

First balaclava helmet

This face-covering woolly hat was invented to keep soldiers warm in the Crimean War of the 1850s.

First flags

Flag-waving began at least 5000 years ago. The oldest national flag is Denmark's, which dates from 1219.

First matchbox labels

The first matches were sold in metal boxes. People began collecting paper labels from matchboxes from the 1830s onwards. There are said to be 40,000 different Swedish matchbox labels.

First Englishman to eat with a fork

Thomas Coryate admired this table refinement while visiting Italy in the 1500s. People in England ate with their fingers or with knives.

First three-million dollar suit

US Shuttle astronauts put on special suits for working outside the spacecraft, or EVA (extra-vehicular activity). Each suit with its built-in life support system costs just over three million dollars to make. Inside the Shuttle, astronauts make do with overalls.

First singing of the Marseillaise

'The Marseillaise', France's national anthem, was written during the French Revolution (in one night, 24 April 1792) by a musical army officer, Claude-Joseph Rouget de Lisle.

DAILY LIFE

Life for our Stone Age ancestors was not all bad. There was no housework, washing, shopping: no papers to read, no doors to lock, no freezers to fill. In summer, when food was plentiful, they probably just lazed around.

First weavers

When people first wove cloth is not known. Wool and linen were woven between 8000 and 7000 years ago. By 5000 years ago, people in India could make cotton cloth.

First dyes

Dyes were first made by crushing up dead insects and animals such as the murex (a sea snail).

First lock and key

Rich people locked their doors with wooden keys 4000 years ago. These locks were cunningly made, but not thief-proof. Metal locks and keys were first used in Ancient Rome.

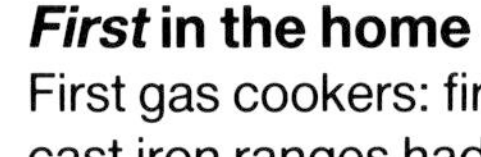

First in the home

First gas cookers: first used in the 1880s, before then cast iron ranges had a coal or wood fire.

First electric fire: bar fires were sold by Belling in 1912.

First successful vacuum cleaner: in 1901, Hubert Booth designed an electric vacuum cleaner that sucked up dust.

First mechanical refrigerator: Jacob Perkins invented the compression refrigerator in 1834.

First sewing machine: After earlier machines were smashed by angry workers this was re-invented by Elias Howe and Isaac Singer (separately) in the 1840s.

◁ Early vacuum cleaner

Food Firsts

First hamburger: 1902 in the USA, introduced by German migrants and named after the German city of Hamburg.

First breakfast cereals: in the 1890s in the USA. Cornflakes were first eaten in 1894.

First Coke: Coca-cola 1886, invented by Dr John Pemberton of Atlanta, Georgia, USA.

First ice-creams: eaten in Roman times, cooled with ice stored in ice-houses.

First vineyards: grapes were first grown in Turkey 4000 years ago. Wine was made from other fruits and berries long before.

First sandwich: said to have been the invention of the Earl of Sandwich (1713–92).

Frozen foods: refrigerated meat shipments began in 1879. Frozen foods was first sold in shops in the 1920s.

First canned food

Nicolas Appert of France solved the problem of feeding an army on the march in the early 1800s. He preserved food by boiling it in sealed jars. The British navy bought canned food for the first time in 1812. But nobody invented a can-opener until the 1860s!

First spectacles
People first used eyeglasses in the 1200s, in China and Europe. Paired lenses came into use in the 1300s. Contact lenses were invented in 1887.

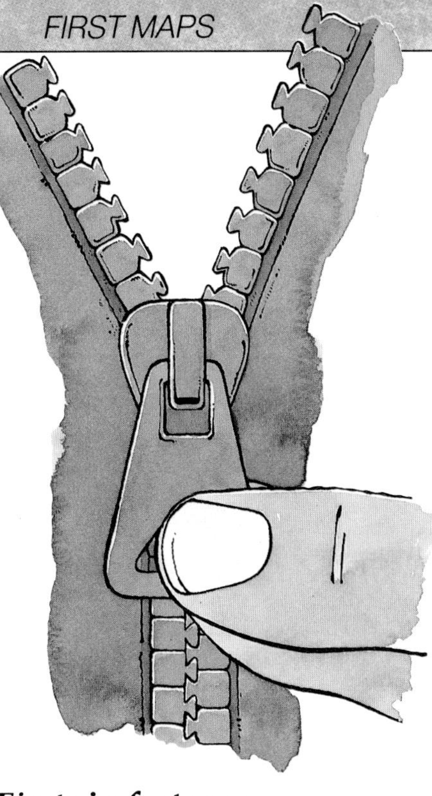

First water closet
Water-flushed lavatories are thousands of years old. But the WC flushed by water piped from the house supply was invented in 1589 by Sir John Harrington.

First maps
The first known map was drawn in Babylon, in about 2500 BC. Printed maps appeared from the 1400s.

First safety matches
Self-lighting matches were invented in Britain in 1827 by John Walker. Safety matches were developed in the 1850s.

First newspapers
The first regularly produced newspapers date from the 1600s in Europe. News pamphlets were printed in Germany as early as 1470. The oldest newspaper still being published is Swedish, and began its 'life' in 1645.

First zip fastener
In 1891, Judson Whitcomb of Chicago, USA designed a new interlocking fastener and called it the zip.

First central heating
Romans kept their villas warm by putting more wood on the hypocaust. Hot air from a furnace circulated under the floor and up through pipes in the walls.

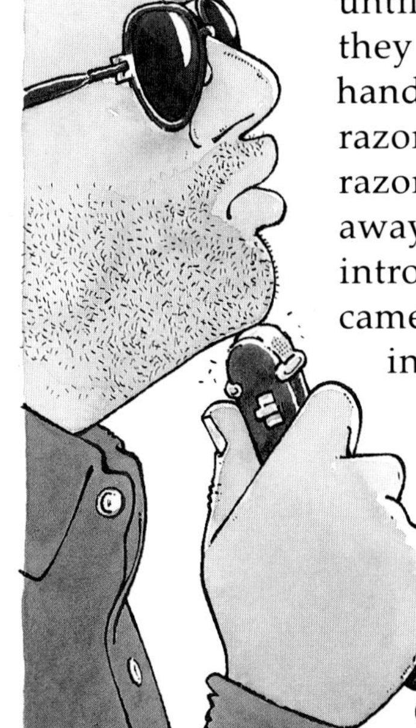

First electric razor
Men scraped their stubble with knives until the 1760s, when they could buy folding-handled 'cut throat' razors. After the safety razor with its throw-away blade was introduced in 1895, came the electric razor in 1931.

First Christmas trees
Protestant reformer Martin Luther is said to have liked Christmas trees. Prince Albert helped make them popular in Britain in the mid-1800s.

First pocket calculator
Adding machines were as big as typewriters before the 1970s. Microelectronics and liquid crystal displays made possible the cheap, battery-powered pocket calculator.

First soap
Soap made from fat and potash mixed was used at least 5000 years ago. Europeans began making soap in the AD 900s. The first soap powders were made in 1845.

INDEX